Praise for *The Hidden Heist*

"*The Hidden Heist* takes you on a thrilling journey while teaching invaluable lessons about money and life. A truly refreshing approach to financial literacy."

Tammy Lally, The Money Coach,
Author of *Money Detox*, and TED Speaker

"Think: Netflix thriller meets *The Only Money Guide You'll Ever Need*. I couldn't put it down. Imagine that; a thoroughly gripping and enjoyable read while learning some game-changing, principle-based wealth-building wisdom. Gift this book to your children and grandchildren and be sure and pick up a copy for yourself. WOW!"

Bob Burg, Coauthor of *The Go-Giver* and Author of *Endless Referrals*

"Bill and Jeff craft an engaging narrative that doubles as a financial playbook, compelling you to reflect, 'Am I serving my present self at the expense of my own future?'"

Chad Hufford, Veritas Wealth Management,
Author of *Forging Financial Freedom*

"Cates and West weave humor and suspense to get us to pay attention to the topic we avoid—our finances. Through a story, we listen without our money biases and learn easy steps to launch a less stressful and more successful money life."

Spencer Sherman, CFP®, MBA
Founder & Advisor, Abacus Wealth and Author of *The Cure for Money Madness*

"*The Hidden Heist* is a brilliantly told story with a powerful message; your money mindset can either rob you or enrich you. Cates and West have crafted a parable that's as entertaining as it is transformative."

Ellen Rogin, CPA, CFP®
New York Times Bestselling Author of
Picture Your Prosperity and *Messages from Money*

"*The Hidden Heist* is more than a story—it's a behavioral breakthrough. Cates and West have cracked the code on making financial wisdom stick, blending timeless lessons with the power of story. It invites readers to confront and rewrite their money scripts in a way that's fresh, relatable, and actionable. A must-read for anyone ready to take ownership of their financial future."

Yohance Harrison, BFA™, CRPC®
Founder & CEO, Money Script Wealth Management

"*The Hidden Heist* is financial storytelling at its finest. Bill Cates and Jeff West don't just teach you about money—they pull you into a page-turner that shifts how you think about building wealth. This isn't just a book—it's a breakthrough."

Derrick Kinney
Bestselling Author, *Good Money Revolution* and Founder, AnyoneCanBecomeAMillionaire.com

"As a psychotherapist and financial wellness expert, I know firsthand how deeply our beliefs and emotions influence our financial outcomes. In *The Hidden Heist*, Cates and West brilliantly unravel the psychological blocks that keep us stuck in scarcity and deliver practical, empowering insights through a story that is equal parts entertaining and transformational. This is not just a book—it's a mirror, a mentor, and a roadmap to reclaiming your financial freedom."

Joyce Marter, LCPC, CSP
Author of *The Financial Mindset Fix: A Mental Fitness Program for an Abundant Life*

"In working with my clients (mostly women)—helping them step into financial freedom with confidence and purpose—it's clear that money is a mindset game. In *The Hidden Heist*, Cates and West bring heart, clarity, and decades of expertise to the table; helping readers break free from limiting beliefs about wealth. The message in this book can be transformational."

Lisa Chastain
Author of *Stop Budgeting Start Living* and Professional Money Coach

"*The Hidden Heist* is a smart, eye-opening guide that exposes the subtle ways people sabotage their own financial futures—and how to stop it. With their signature blend of storytelling and strategy, Bill Cates and Jeff C. West reveal the 'hidden thieves' that steal wealth over time, from poor habits to misguided beliefs. This book doesn't just offer advice—it empowers readers to take back control, build lasting wealth, and live with greater financial intention. A must-read for anyone ready to stop leaving money on the table and start building a life of abundance."

Cary Carbonaro, MBA, CFP®
Award-Winning Financial Advisor and Author of *Women and Wealth*

"*The Hidden Heist* blends suspense with actionable advice on overcoming financial obstacles—a must-read for anyone striving for independence. I just love how the authors wove their excellent financial advice into a page-turning story!"

Lisa M. Wilber
Top 5 Leader with Avon U.S. (over twenty years),
Speaker, and Coauthor of *Said the Lady with the Blue Hair*

"Are you confident about your current financial situation? Could your beliefs and attitudes toward money be holding you back? Women grow up being told not to worry their pretty heads about money. Sound familiar? If so, then *The Hidden Heist*, written by Bill Cates and Jeff C. West, is a must-read. This engaging and entertaining parable will help you uncover the mental blocks that may be limiting your financial potential—and show you how to achieve the success you deserve and desire."

Susan Solovic
THE Small Business Expert, TV Personality,
and *New York Times* Bestselling Author

"*The Hidden Heist* is a brilliant and entertaining roadmap to financial clarity. Through compelling storytelling, Cates and West reveal the mindset shifts and practical steps that can help anyone reclaim control of their financial future. As a CFP® professional, I see daily how powerful a shift in beliefs can be—and this book delivers that message in a way that truly resonates. A must-read for anyone ready to stop robbing themselves and start building real wealth."

Misty Lynch, CFP®
CEO of Sound View Financial Advisors
& Host of *Demystifying Money* Podcast

THE HIDDEN HEIST

Stop Robbing Yourself of Lasting Wealth

(An Irresistible Tale of Financial Redemption)

Bill Cates, CSP, CPAE & Jeff C. West

THUNDER HILL PRESS

Copyright © 2025 by Bill Cates and Jeff C. West

All rights reserved. Except as permitted under the United States Copyright Act of 1976, no part of this publication may be reproduced or distributed in any form or by any means, or stored in a database or retrieval system, without the prior written permission of both the authors and the publisher. If you would like to quote from, excerpt, or otherwise use material from this book, please contact billcates@referralcoach.com

Thunder Hill Press
705 Childs Point Road
Suite 102
Annapolis, MD 21401

Printed in the United States of America

First Edition: September 2025

Produced by GMK Writing and Editing, Inc.
Managing Editor: Katie Benoit
Copyedited by Josh Rosenberg
Proofread by Elizabeth Crooks
Cover design and text design by Vicky Vaughn Shea
Composition by Joanna Beyer

Hardcover ISBN: 978-1-888970-09-8
Paperback ISBN: 978-1-888970-10-4
eBook EISN: 978-1-888970-11-1
Audiobook: 978-1-888970-12-8

Visit the authors at: www.ReferralCoach.com and www.jeffcwest.com

Library of Congress Control Number: 2025912875

Limit of liability disclaimer of warranty: *While the authors and book producer have used their best efforts in preparing this book, they make no representations or warranties with respect to the accuracy or completeness of the contents of this book and specifically disclaim any implied warranties of merchantability or fitness for a particular purpose. The advice and strategies contained herein may not be suitable for your situation. Neither the publisher nor authors shall be liable for any loss of profit or any other financial damages, including, but not limited, to special incidental, consequential, or other damages.*

This is a work of fiction. Names, characters, places, events, and incidents are either products of the authors' imagination or used in a fictitious manner. Any resemblance to actual persons, living or dead, or to real events is purely coincidental.

The views and opinions expressed by the characters do not necessarily reflect those of the authors. This book is intended for entertainment purposes only.

To every human being who desires to have a healthy relationship with money—to understand money and use it to better themselves and all they touch.

~ Bill Cates, CSP, CPAE

To all those who have struggled with their relationship with money. If we can change that relationship, so can you.
~ Jeff C. West

CONTENTS

Acknowledgments xi
Foreword by John David Mann xiii
Preface – Unlocking Prosperity: Knowledge Meets
    Self-Awareness xvii
Introduction – Money's Power: A Choice We Make xix
Chapter 1 – The Perils of Poor Planning 1
Chapter 2 – A Fox Among the Chickens 7
Chapter 3 – How Would *You* Know, Mr. Beckett? 17
Chapter 4 – A Victimless Crime? 27
Chapter 5 – Into the River of Money 37
Chapter 6 – The Hidden Heist of False Perceptions 51
Chapter 7 – Secrets in the Vault 65
Chapter 8 – Become Financially Literate 71
Chapter 9 – Misguided Stereotypes 79
Chapter 10 – It's You, Isn't It? 93
Chapter 11 – The Value of a Financial Professional 99
Chapter 12 – Financial Independence, One Law at a Time 107
Chapter 13 – Breaking Free 119
Chapter 14 – Multiple Streams, Greater Dreams 131
Chapter 15 – All Good Things 139
Epilogue – The Best Gift I've Ever Received 145
Appendix I – Limiting Beliefs, Mistaken Assumptions,
    and Unhelpful Emotions 151
Appendix II – Wealthy Mindset and Action Steps for
    Financial Independence 157
Appendix III – Eight Strategies to Grow and Protect Your
    Financial Future 161

Unlock THE VAULT
And Your Financial Independence

Secure the **combination** to access your FREE Resources

Visit **HiddenHeistVault.com**
to claim your exclusive access to The Vault - a treasure trove of guides and insights designed to help you:

- Enrich your money mindset
- Grow lasting personal wealth
- Avoid financial regrets
- Move toward financial freedom

Inside The Vault, you will discover powerful resources like:

- 9 Strategies to Grow and Protect Your Financial Future
- How Ordinary People Become Millionaires
- 13 Important Things You Can Do With Money
- Can Money Buy Happiness? Think Twice
- The Ever-Flowing River of Money
- Creating Generational Wealth
- **Behind the Scenes: Interviews with Bill, Jeff, and some special guests who... well...let's just say have first-hand experience in the world of hostage negotiations.**

Your journey to a wiser, wealthier life starts here.

 Go to **www.HiddenHeistVault.com** to unlock the combination today!

ACKNOWLEDGMENTS

A heartfelt thank-you to our friends and colleagues who generously shared their beliefs and experiences about money, their guidance on storyline and content, and reviewed earlier versions of the manuscript to contribute their wisdom. Your help is greatly appreciated. You made this a better book.

Bob Burg, Jessica Cates-Bristol, Shirley Davis, Randy Gage, Michael Goldberg, Scott Halford, Yohance Harrison, Abbey Henderson, Pat Hogan, Myah Irick, John Johnson, Willie Jolley, Zermira Jones, Tammy Lally, John Landry, Marissa Levin, Mark Lowther, Misty Lynch, John David Mann, Machen MacDonald, Taylor Maks, Dennis O'Keefe, Suzi Pomerantz, Randy Richie, Ellen Rogin, Mike Schmidtmann, Allison Shapira, Alice Tang, Russ Thornton, Erin Willis, and William Wright.

FOREWORD

It's easy to write a parable.

Wait—scratch that. It's easy to write a *bad* parable. It's hard to write a good one. And a great one? That's fiendishly difficult.

Before I tell you that the book you hold in your hand (or gaze at on your iPad or have playing in your ear) is one of the great ones, let me tell you why.

There are three essential ingredients that go into making a parable work. The first is *worthy insight*. The second is *clear writing*. And the third . . . well, I'll save the third for last.

For insight to be "worthy" means it has genuine worth: value that you can actually use, and will—and not only that, but when you do it will make a significant difference in your life. For that, neither information nor knowledge will do the job. Information you can get on Google; for knowledge, there's YouTube. For a parable to be worthy, it has to bring you wisdom.

Wisdom, as opposed to mere knowledge, offers principles that are at the same time simple, practical, and timeless. Wisdom is knowledge in context; knowledge put into perspective; knowledge that has been kilned through the fires of experience.

Which brings us to Bill Cates. You can pick up the details of Bill's c.v. and qualifications by turning to the "About the Authors" page. What I'll say here is that I'd rather get my financial wisdom from a guy who has not only written and taught about it extensively and demonstrated it in his own business and consultancy, but who has also trekked the Andes and Himalayas, scaled the summit of Kilimanjaro, camped out in the Arctic Circle, and toured the U.S. of A. as the drummer of a rock band.

It's the life experience thing. A.I. is never gonna give you that.

The second thing a parable needs is *clear writing*. Writing that is immaculately clean, concise, and compelling.

A parable is an epic in microcosm, a novel in a nutshell. In these pages, you'll never learn what color Alden Beckett's hair is, or who his parents were, or whether he ever had a drinking problem. Novels do that; a parable has to cut to the chase—yet do so in a way that is engaging, entertaining, even at points emotionally moving. There is a skill to that; actually, a whole set of skills.

Which brings us to Jeff C. West.

Jeff already had three home runs under his belt by the time he and Bill teamed up to write *The Hidden Heist*. Jeff's first parable, written solo, won the prestigious Axiom Business Book Award's bronze medal. His second, written with Avon superstar Lisa Wilber, took Axiom silver. And his third with my *Go-Giver* coauthor Bob Burg? Maybe you've already guessed. Yep: the gold. With each outing, Jeff's skill set has gotten sharper and sharper . . . and with this book, even sharper.

What's beyond gold? We'll call it platinum.

The third thing a parable needs to work is *authentic humanity*.

People learn through stories, and for a story to work, it has to draw you in. If the characters are cardboard cutouts, shallow stand-ins for points the author wants to make, the story devolves into a thinly veiled PowerPoint. We need to care about these characters and what happens to them, because if we don't resonate with their story, we don't get drawn in and the wisdom doesn't stick.

Even in the simplest of fables, for the thing to work, the characters have to be real. Think of Aesop's cocksure hare and plodding tortoise. The flawed brothers of the Prodigal Son parable; the sanctimonious priest and Levite from the parable of the Good Samaritan. Even stubborn Hem and affable Haw, the "little people" from *Who Moved My Cheese?*, are strikingly human and distinct from one another.

In *The Hidden Heist* you'll meet and fall in love with (or at the very least, in fascination with) Alden Beckett, the man with a mysterious past who knows more than he should; Carl, whose quick temper serves to cover a deepening desperation; conflicted Bobby, who's got a story of his own to hide; quick-witted Gabrielle, one of only three female SWAT team commanders in the Lone Star State; and a dozen others, every one as unforgettable as the last.

And have I mentioned the ingenious setting where this all takes place?

Pat Lencioni sets his parables in realistic business settings. David Bach and I opened *The Latte Factor* in the heart of New York City's financial district at 9/11's ground zero. Spencer Johnson put his two mice and two mouse-sized dudes in the heart of a maze in an undisclosed location, like a parabolic rendition.

But Bill and Jeff have done something I'd never seen before, and I'm pretty sure I'll never see again: They've set their parable at the point of a gun, in a vault in the midst of a bank robbery. Jeff calls it "*The Breakfast Club* meets *Dog Day Afternoon*, only funnier."

Its humor is undeniable—and so is its wisdom.

—John David Mann
Coauthor of *The Go-Giver* series with Bob Burg and coauthor of *The Latte Factor* with David Bach

PREFACE

Unlocking Prosperity: Knowledge Meets Self-Awareness

I believe that every human being deserves to make educated financial decisions that are in their best interest. This belief has turned into my mission.

For 30 years, I've helped financial professionals of many types attract and serve more clients—guiding those clients in making crucial decisions around money. In that way, I have furthered my mission. While I continue to serve financial professionals with my systems to attract the right clients for them, this book marks a significant step in the expansion of my mission—directly reaching more individuals with perspectives and action steps to build a healthier relationship with money.

To my mind there are two key steps to improve our relationship with money. The first is education, often called financial literacy. Knowing how money works can have a significant impact on one's ability to make better money decisions. The other is self-awareness, especially understanding how our limiting beliefs and mistaken assumptions shape our relationship with money. By gaining knowledge and reshaping our mindset, we put ourselves in place to develop better beliefs, feelings, and actions (above all—the right actions). From there, we can grow our wealth and achieve financial independence, for ourselves, those we care about, and even future generations.

—**Bill Cates,** CSP, CPAE

Over the years, I have witnessed countless people make two big money mistakes. First, they believed wealth-building was reserved for "other people"—not them. Second, they had no real plan for how they handled their money day to day.

The result? Financial stress that lasted for years, strained relationships—often ending with broken marriages, and families struggling unnecessarily.

So, when one of my heroes, Bill Cates, suggested we write a parable together about the myths, missteps, and mindset shifts needed for financial success, I didn't hesitate. (In fact, I might have said "yes" before he finished his sentence.)

This book is not about get-rich-quick schemes or complicated financial jargon. It's about real, practical habits that can change your financial future. And since stories stick with us far better than lectures, we wrapped these lessons in a tale that I hope you will find entertaining, insightful, and maybe even a little unforgettable.

My wish for you, dear reader, is that this story sparks a shift in how you think about money—and that you put these principles into action to create a future that's not just financially secure but truly fulfilling.

Enjoy the journey!

—Jeff C. West

INTRODUCTION

Money's Power: A Choice We Make

This book is an invitation to rethink everything you believe about money. To challenge the assumptions that have held you back. To replace fear with knowledge, scarcity with abundance, and financial stress with financial empowerment.

Let's get started . . .

Money is neither good nor bad—it simply is.

Money has value only because we, as a society, have agreed that it does. That agreement brings with it a belief system that is woven into every aspect of human life. It facilitates trade, represents stored value, and enables the exchange of goods and services. But beyond its practical function, money carries deep psychological and emotional weight.

Long before paper bills and digital transactions, societies depended on the barter system—exchanging goods and services directly. But over time, money changed from its early form—including shells, livestock, and metals—to that of coins and paper. Today, digital wallet, peer-to-peer, tap your credit card, and cryptocurrencies push the evolution of money even further.

But no matter the form, money only holds the power we give to it.

The Invisible Chains of Money Beliefs

Despite money's inherent neutrality, our relationship with it is anything but. From childhood, many of us adopt limiting beliefs about money, absorbing messages from parents, teachers, and the media. *"Money doesn't grow on trees." "Rich people are greedy." "I'll never make enough."* These beliefs become so deeply embedded that we mistake them for absolute truths, unknowingly allowing them to dictate our financial behaviors and, ultimately, our financial outcomes.

Agreed, money does not grow on trees (unless you're an apple farmer) and yes, some rich people are greedy. Yet many of these long-held beliefs about money are mistaken, creating invisible barriers to financial success. As a result, we fear scarcity, even when opportunities are abundant. We equate self-worth with net worth, leading to stress, anxiety, and poor decision-making. We avoid financial discussions out of discomfort, leaving us ill-equipped to manage and grow our wealth.

But what if we could change our relationship with money? What if we intentionally rewrote that script? How would our lives and the lives of those around us change?

Choosing a New Financial Mindset

The truth is money only has the power we believe it has. We have a choice in how we think, feel, and act regarding money. We can remain shackled by outdated, limiting beliefs, or we can embrace new perspectives that open us up to financial success and independence—recognizing that money is a tool—not a source of identity, not an object of fear.

We can use money wisely. We can approach it with confidence rather than avoidance, make informed financial decisions, and create lasting wealth. True financial independence is not just about earning more or spending less; it's about aligning our financial actions with our values and goals.

You have a choice. You can continue to operate under the old system of inherited beliefs and self-imposed limitations, or you can take control, transform your mindset, and set yourself free.

The choice is yours. This book will aid you in this choice and your journey to building lasting wealth and financial independence.

And now . . . on with the story.

"Money is meant to be used, and people are meant to be loved. Trouble starts when we reverse the two."

—Alden Beckett

CHAPTER 1

The Perils of Poor Planning

9:05 a.m.

"Everybody on the floor!"

An eerie silence enveloped the lobby of Community Savings and Loan. No one moved. No one talked. Everyone stared in confused disbelief.

Chak-chak.

The distinctive sound of the pump-action shotgun left no doubt—this was a serious situation.

"I said everybody on the floor!"

The security guard, the bank manager, and the lady sitting in front of the manager's desk dropped onto the cold tile; two customers who had just reached the counter did likewise. The teller continued to stand, closely watching the men. Her hand crept under the counter toward the silent alarm button.

The man with the shotgun turned and shouted, "No! You don't wanna do that!"

She eased her hand back onto the counter, walked around front, and joined the others.

Everyone kept their heads down.

Everyone, that is, except Alden Beckett.

Alden didn't move. He remained sitting where he was, simply staring at the three men who'd entered the bank five minutes after the door was unlocked.

They wore black BDUs—Battle Dress Uniforms—their faces concealed with ninja-style black head coverings. While this may have looked quite intimidating on the big screen, on these three guys, the outfits looked more clownish than scary.

Maybe it was because of their eye coverings. Full-rimmed mirrored sunglasses hid the eyes of two of the robbers, and a pair of prescription swim-goggles covered those of the third, making his eyes appear distorted—like those of an enormous fish.

Other than the goggle-distorted brown eyes of the one, there were no visible identifying marks.

The tall man—not Fish Eyes, but the one with the shotgun—pivoted to the right and looked at Alden. He pointed the weapon toward him, keeping the barrel pointed slightly off to the left and down.

That's nice of him. Don't want that Remington 870 pointed my way. Always treat a gun as if it's loaded, even when it's not.

The man yelled, "What's wrong with you? I told you—get down on the floor!"

Alden laughed.

Not because he was an exceptionally brave man. Although he'd certainly seen dangerous situations before. Not because he had some perverse wish to force the man to shoot him, such as those times when criminals saw no other way out of their dilemma, and committed "suicide by cop." And not even because of the way the men carried themselves—clumsy, clueless, and looking at each other for signs of what to do next. One even dropped his handgun and quickly retrieved it—holding the barrel toward his own chest.

Okay. Ninjas, they're not.

Alden knew he wasn't watching a well-oiled tactical unit. Instead, he was watching three incompetent would-be criminals attempting their first bank robbery.

Moe, Larry, and Curly, he thought, failing to stifle his chuckle.

Moe, the one with the shotgun, screamed, "Are you crazy?"

Alden stopped laughing, at least on the outside. But his grin remained.

Why *had* he been so amused?

First, he had a keen eye for detail, and earlier, as the tall man racked the forestock, Alden saw directly into the action of the shotgun.

It wasn't loaded.

And second, this enraged man was obviously the leader of the crew—the cream of the criminal crop. And the brilliant architect of this morning's heist, which would undoubtedly become this evening's news, had failed to comprehend the significance of one simple thing.

Alden was a paraplegic, sitting in a wheelchair, and unable to move anything from the waist down.

"Why are you smiling?" thundered Moe, moving a step closer.

Alden lifted both hands and said, "Dude, I'm in a wheelchair. I couldn't get down on the ground if I wanted to. What do you *expect* me to do?"

Alden could indeed get down on the floor. Other than moving his legs, he was completely adept at doing anything he needed to. He had tremendous upper body strength, and for a man of his age, was in great shape. He didn't really consider himself handicapped.

Still, he was confident that these Three Stooges wouldn't question the extent of his dexterity. So, he decided not to get his clothes dirty.

Moe growled and moved toward Alden.

"Arghhhhhhhhh!"

Alden braced himself for what was to come. Moe couldn't shoot him, but he fully expected a shotgun stock to the face, or to be dumped over sideways onto the ground by a very pissed-off villain.

Just before Moe reached the wheelchair, bank robber number two, a.k.a. Larry, the one wearing the goggles, raced between them.

"Carl! No!"

Moe, or now maybe Carl, halted. Even more angry, he spewed his words.

"What the hell, Jamie? Carl? Really?"

Okay, definitely Carl.

Not that they couldn't have come up with aliases to use if needed. But Alden was reasonably sure these men hadn't planned that far ahead. Still, he needed to be cautious. A high IQ wasn't required for someone to cause harm, a truth he carried with him daily.

So . . . Carl: 6'3", muscular shoulders, Southern accent, the leader of the group. Larry—now Jamie: brown eyes, 5'9", 20 pounds overweight . . . maybe 200 pounds, also with a Southern accent. Curly: 6'2" or so . . . lean.

Jamie said, "Well, the way you were going at him, I thought if I called you 'Barney,' or something, you wouldn't have known I was talking to you."

Interesting. This one may be smarter than the rest.

"You're an idiot," shouted Carl. "No names! We said that for a reason!"

"I know, I know. It just came out."

"I can't believe you did that!"

Jamie gestured toward the third robber. "Well, they still don't know Bobby's name!"

Scratch that. Jamie's not the brighter bulb after all. Curly is now Bobby.

"Excuse me," Alden said. "May I ask you a question?"

"No!" the two men shouted in unison.

"It's kind of important."

"No!" both shouted again and returned to their bickering.

"Okay." He held up the cell phone he'd removed from a leather bag attached to his chair during their spat. Alden asked, "But what should I tell the 911 operator?"

The two men immediately stopped.

"911. What is the nature of your emergency?"

Nobody said a word.

"911. Please state the nature of your emergency."

Carl walked over to Alden and grabbed the cell phone.

Calming his voice, but glaring at Alden, Carl said, "Sorry, operator. No emergency here. Butt-dial."

Carl then shut down the phone, dropped it onto the floor, and crushed it with his boot.

"You know," said Alden, "it's standard practice for an interrupted 911 call to receive an immediate response, don't you? The police will be here in about eight minutes. You may want to get the hell out now."

"How do *you* know so much about police procedure?" barked Carl.

"I watch a lot of cop shows on TV."

I wonder if he bought that?

Alden wasn't certain what the local response time would be today. But he knew this merry band of robbers would be clueless. He thought the bluff might just work and get the men to exit.

Carl said, "Listen, smart guy! Roll yourself over there by . . ."

"By Bobby?" Alden smiled.

Carl fumed. "Just . . . go!"

Alden made his way over to the others, as Jamie and Carl whispered. Bobby, the robber formerly known as Curly, stayed completely quiet and still. He kept his eyes fixed on the group on the floor.

Carl and Jamie grew louder—arguing over their next move.

Alden couldn't hear them clearly.

There's no way these guys planned anything for this contingency. Ahh, the perils of poor planning. Wish I had taken that lip-reading class, now.

Their discussion, as well as their decision-making process, ground to a sudden halt with the sound of a police siren—now in the distance but getting closer and more blaring by the second.

"Alright, everybody! Listen up," said Carl. "Get your cell phones out and give them to . . ."

"To Bobby," Jamie pointed, without hesitation.

Carl seethed. "To Bobby!"

"This was supposed to be a quick, in-and-out, bank robbery. Grab the cash and disappear." Pointing to Alden, Carl said, "But now, thanks to this guy, we have a full-blown hostage situation here!"

The third bank robber, Bobby, dropped his head. He muttered, "I can't believe this is happening."

CHAPTER 2

A Fox Among the Chickens

9:15 a.m.

Bobby's relationship with finances had always been turbulent. His attitude toward money kept him broke and in constant conflict with his wife. He'd been living paycheck to overdraft for decades. Never being able to get ahead, Bobby often felt like a financial hostage, unable to escape his captors of credit card debt and lack of resources.

In a desperate move, he'd agreed to be part of this heist to bankroll his rent for the month.

Just half an hour ago, as the three men sat in the car, putting on their disguises, Bobby rocked back into his seat, realizing his mistake. *I have no business doing this. I'm no bank robber.*

Now, 15 minutes into the caper, the whole scenario had degraded into a complete snafu.

Every terrible choice Bobby had made dropped him squarely into the front seat of this thrill ride, like a rollercoaster slowly clicking up toward the first lift hill.

He regretted his decision and wanted to hop out of the seat. However, events were in motion, the lap bar was down, and there was no way he could escape.

Bobby walked over to Carl and whispered, "Listen. Nobody needs to get hurt here. Keep a cool head, okay?"

Carl said, "Just shut up and do your job."

Carl turned his attention to the security guard. "Give me the keys to the door."

The guard kept her face to the ground. "They're clipped to my belt,"—which was next to her gun. "Do you want me to get them, or would you rather I keep my hands where they are?"

Alden was glad to hear how the guard responded. Not surprised. Just happy to see the exchange.

He'd known the woman, Yen Giang, for over two years now, and respected her. Though only in her mid-30s, she was mature beyond her years. Contrary to pop culture and movies, most security guards don't have an "I'm taking that fool out, first chance I get" mentality. Instead, especially when the criminal has the upper hand and innocent bystanders are around, they're much more interested in defusing the situation. They don't care to throw C-4 onto a rocket launcher. At least that had been true for the security guards Alden had known. And Yen definitely belonged in that group. She'd once told him her name, Yen, was Vietnamese for "calm and safe."

Nice job, Yen. Calm. Non-confrontational. Living up to your name very well. Glad it's you in here with us. The shotgun's not loaded. Not sure about the others. Better safe than sorry.

Carl nodded to Jamie, keeping his weapon pointed toward the guard.

Jamie didn't move.

Carl nodded again.

Jamie shrugged.

Carl jabbed his finger toward the guard. "Get the keys, you idiot!"

"Oh. Sorry."

Jamie reached down to the guard's belt and unclipped her keys.

"Get her gun, too," said Carl.

Yen noticed Jamie's hands trembling. "It's okay, Jamie. Relax. Nobody in here's going to give you any problems. We all want to make it out safely."

"Thanks," said Jamie. "I'm just so nervous, ya know? I appreciate you being so nice . . ."

"Aww. How sweet," said Carl. "Are you two through with your counseling session here?"

Jamie said, "Well, it wasn't actually a counseling session." He forced a laugh. "I mean, *she's* not my . . ." He cleared his throat. "I mean, she's not a counselor."

He glanced at Carl's face and quickly added, "Yes. We're through now."

Carl took Yen's gun from Jamie, tucked it inside his belt, and yelled, "Now go lock the doors!"

"Okay! Alright already! I'm going!"

Carl said, "And find something to jam between the handles!"

Jamie scurried to the front door and locked it. He unhooked one of the red velvet stanchion ropes from the teller's cue line, ran it back and forth between the handles, and clipped the ends together.

Once finished, he looked out through the glass.

A single police car had parked out front. The officer took cover behind his open door. Staring directly at Jamie, he tucked his chin, pressed the button on his shoulder mic and began speaking into it.

Jamie sprinted back to Carl.

"A cop's out there already! He called it in!"

Carl grinned and looked at their seven captives. "Don't worry. For now, at least, we've got the upper hand."

Everyone continued to keep their faces buried—except one. Alden Beckett.

Carl's eyes locked on Alden's.

Neither man blinked.

Neither man spoke.

The criminal team captain walked up to Alden, his stride deliberate and slow.

"There's something about you . . . something I *really* don't like." Moving to within inches of Alden's face, Carl whispered, "Me not liking you ain't a good idea. At least not for you."

Alden whispered back. "Seriously? Carl, I'm sorry. It's probably just something you're not used to seeing. Maybe it's the chair. My charming wit? My full set of teeth?"

Carl spoke louder, and everyone in the room could hear. "I can remove some of those teeth, smart ass. Stay out of my way and cause no problems. You understand?"

Alden said nothing. After a moment, he lifted his hands in consent.

Bobby nodded for the crew to move away from Alden and toward the front of the lobby. *Gotta keep Carl calm. Gotta get these people somewhere safe.*

Bobby whispered to Carl and Jamie. Carl looked back at the people on the floor and nodded.

"Alright, get up," said Carl. "Everybody's going into the vault."

No one moved. They simply lifted their faces and stared.

"Now!"

The group rose cautiously and walked toward the open door.

Alden said, "There's something you should know."

Carl didn't reply. He tilted his head, dropped his eyes, and glared at Alden.

That's too funny. He's giving me "the look," but doesn't remember—I can't see his eyes.

Alden said, "If you're going to put us in there, you may want to leave the door open. Later, when they cut the electricity, the vault will automatically lock. The air won't last long."

Alden crinkled his nose and shook his head. "You don't want this to escalate to that level, right?"

Carl sighed. "How do you *know* these things?"

"It's in all the Bruce Willis movies." Alden's brows rose.

Carl said nothing.

Alden bit his lip. *Don't smile now. He's still not figuring this one out. Advantage, Beckett.*

Alden didn't actually believe the SWAT team, which was certain to arrive, would shut off the electricity. And even if they did, vaults were ventilated.

Yes, they would likely kill the water to create some discomfort for these comic-strip villains. They'd stop the gas to avoid potential hazardous issues with an unexpected leak. Cell phones in the building would be pinged, then turned off for sure. And they would put the landlines on ringdown, limiting communications to only the lieutenant in charge anytime someone picked up the handset. Allowing these three miscreant musketeers to contact wives, girlfriends, or the media would not be acceptable to SWAT command.

However, the electricity would likely stay on.

Not for the comfort of those inside the bank. But to give police a direct line of sight into the lobby. The bank had security cameras in all four corners, and two additional lenses behind the teller stations. When SWAT contacted the bank's corporate office, they would gain immediate access to the live feed.

"Okay," said Carl. "Bobby, put them in the vault, but leave the door open. Then you stand guard there. Nobody goes in or out. Understand?"

Bobby nodded.

Alden asked, "Is it alright if they take chairs in?" He motioned to his chair. "I don't want to be the only one lavishing in luxury."

Carl agreed, and each hostage grabbed a chair and moved into the vault.

Alden stopped at the door and asked Bobby, "Mind if I stay here in the doorway? I'm a little claustrophobic."

Bobby signaled agreement.

Alden moved into position, making sure he could see both the vault and the lobby.

"Thanks, Bobby. I appreciate it."

Hmm. Bobby's not like the other two. Quiet. Observant. Calm. Maybe he's the most intelligent of the three.

Bobby puzzled Alden. He didn't quite fit in with Carl and Jamie.

"You really don't want this to get out of hand," said Alden. "Do you?"

Bobby said nothing. *You have no idea.*

Alden started to speak. But he decided to let the issue drop . . . for now.

Alden turned his attention to the rest of the hostages. "You may as well get comfortable, folks. We're gonna be in here for a while. It'll probably be 30 minutes to an hour before the police even establish contact."

Bobby almost spoke but only stared. *How does he know this?*

Alden noticed his slight head movement. "What?"

Bobby slowly shook his head.

"You're wondering how I know that too, aren't you?" said Alden.

Bobby gave a single nod. *Okay. He's perceptive. I'll give him that.*

Alden laughed. "It's YouTube! You can learn anything there!"

Bobby didn't laugh.

"What? Not even a chuckle? You gotta admit—that was funny!"

Turning to the others, Alden said, "Bank robbers apparently have no sense of humor these days."

Bobby sighed. *I'm no bank robber. At least I wasn't until today.*

As those inside the vault were getting settled, the SWAT team arrived, led by Lieutenant Gabrielle Layton. She was well seasoned and respected, as both a hostage negotiator and commander, for the Washington County SWAT team.

In larger cities, that rare combination of responsibilities would never be coupled. There's an unwritten law enforcement axiom: Commanders never negotiate, and negotiators never command. It's considered a fixed doctrine. However, in Gabrielle's case, small-town budgets equated to fewer officers on the ground and double duty was not unusual.

Gabrielle was skilled and well qualified for both positions.

She began her career in the Dallas County Sheriff's Department. Though she'd loved the work in Dallas, the pace was incredibly fast, and the danger level seemed to rise with each edition of the evening news.

So, to reduce her stress and raise the quality of life for her family, she accepted a position in the much smaller Washington County

Sheriff's Office in Brenham, Texas. An old mentor had contacted her, announcing his retirement, and encouraged her to seek the job.

Gabrielle was only 5 feet tall but was solid muscle. And she was already making a name for herself as one of only three female SWAT team commanders in Texas.

She stepped through the door of the Command van, allowed her eyes to adjust to the darkness for a couple of seconds, then moved toward the tiny desk against the armor-plated wall.

Gabrielle peeked over the shoulder of her second-in-command, Michael Kooper, to get a look at his laptop. "Water off?"

"Yep."

"Gas?"

"Yep."

"Leave the electric on. Has anyone talked with the bank's corporate office?"

"Yep. The live feed'll come through in the next few minutes."

"Do we know how many perps and how many civilians?"

"We think three perps—armed. And six or seven civilians. Won't know for sure 'til we connect to the security cameras."

"CCTV?"

"Workin' on it now. We'll check to see if we can find their car and run the plates."

"How about cell phones?"

"Pinged 'em first. Then turned 'em off."

Gabrielle took the seat beside Kooper. He turned his laptop so she could see the screen. "Here's the list of phones and their owners."

Gabrielle tapped the list with her finger. "Which of these made the 911 call?"

"Neither." He clicked a different tab on his screen. "Emergency dispatch said this is the number that called. I couldn't ping it. It's off now."

"Any idea why?"

"My guess is the robbers destroyed it. I'll run it separately to see whose it is."

Gabrielle leaned closer and peered at the screen. Then laughed.

"What's so funny?"

"You don't need to run that one. I know the number. Looks like the SWAT angels are working with us today."

Kooper frowned. "SWAT angels?"

Gabrielle said, "Alden Beckett."

He laughed and said, "Interesting."

"Interesting for us," said Gabrielle. "A total pain in the ass for the bank robbers."

Kooper grinned. "A fox among the chickens. And they'll never see it coming."

"Greed and financial despair are actually two sides of the same scarcity mindset coin."

—Alden Beckett

CHAPTER 3

How Would *You* Know, Mr. Beckett?

10:00 a.m.

Snow and ice are extremely rare in southeast Texas, but not impossible. As a matter of fact, a winter storm had passed through the Brenham area overnight and dropped a "devastating" half-inch of ice, and a light dusting of snow.

In most parts of the United States, such minuscule amounts of winter precipitation cause no disruption. But in Texas, schools, workplaces, and churches often closed when such "massive" weather events made their way through.

Earlier that morning, an old friend from New Hampshire teased Alden about how Texas responds to even the slightest winter precipitation.

"Aww. Will you guys be okay?" The question oozed sarcasm.

"Eventually," laughed Alden. "In time, we *will* rebuild."

Alden had taken off his gloves and stored them in the pockets of his brown leather coat upon first entering the bank. As he removed his jacket, he saw the teller, Cordelia Ainsworth, sitting in her chair, shivering.

Cordelia was a local Brenham girl. She started working at the bank immediately after graduating from Texas A&M. She'd been homecoming queen at Brenham High, and the bank customers liked and knew her well.

She whimpered.

Alden rolled over to her and draped his coat around her shoulders.

"Hey. It's going to be okay," he whispered. "We're all getting out of here in one piece."

"How do you know?" she asked—eyes leaking.

"That's right!" said the young man who'd walked in just before the robbery began. "The way you keep smartin' off to those guys, you could get us all killed! What makes you think you know so much?"

Before Alden could speak, the bank manager leaned forward, trying to keep his voice down so Bobby couldn't overhear. "Mr. Beckett *would* know . . ."

Alden caught the manager's eyes and discreetly shook his head.

The branch manager stopped.

Alden asked, "What's your name?"

"Dylan. Dylan Bender."

"Mind if I call you Dylan?"

"No."

"Great. Dylan, I'm Alden Beckett."

Alden nodded toward Bobby. "These guys are already making you feel unsafe. I apologize for making you feel even worse. As we go forward, I'll try to keep that in mind."

Dylan nodded.

Alden leaned in and whispered, "I actually *have* had some exposure to people like this before. These guys? Not professionals. Not competent. And they didn't come in here planning to hurt anybody." He looked around the room. "It's okay to relax and stay calm."

Bobby stepped closer. *Not competent—no kidding. Carl even forgot the money, and I'm not going to remind him.*

Alden leaned back in his chair. *Alright. Time to change the subject.*

"Why don't we all get to know each other? Hello everybody, my name's Alden."

In unison, the group said, "Hi Alden."

"Good grief!" said Ayisha Holmes, the second customer of the day. "We sound like a 12-step group for recovering hostage victims." She waved. "Hi. I'm Ayisha."

Alden laughed. He had attended several "Friends of Bill" meetings in the past, where "friends of Alden's" in law enforcement received their sobriety chips. Though their stories were different, they all had two things in common. They were successfully dealing with their recovery, and they had a sense of humor about their journey.

The branch manager sat back in his chair. "I'm Eddie. Eddie Belkin. I'm the bank manager."

"I'm Yen Giang," said the security guard.

"Cordelia," said the teller. "Cordelia Ainsworth."

Dylan waved his hand halfheartedly. "Dylan Bender."

The lady who'd been sitting at the branch manager's desk said nothing.

"Miss?" Alden asked. "Want to tell us your name, too?"

The petite redhead, Cacey Franklin, moved her eyes from Alden, over to Bobby, and quickly back.

She shook her head.

"It's okay. Everybody's a little nervous. You don't have to tell anyone your name if you don't want to."

"Maybe just a first name?" Alden winked. "Might make you feel better . . . the rest of us, too."

Cacey tilted her head down slightly and sighed.

After a moment, she lifted her eyes.

"Cacey." She was barely audible.

Alden said nothing. He just nodded.

Surveying the room, Alden made eye contact with each member of the group. "Why don't we just think of this as friends having lunch together? It'll help pass the time."

Ayisha laughed. "Right . . . friends having lunch together . . . at ten o'clock in the morning . . . in a bank vault . . . with no food. Sounds perfect." She sighed, "I'm on a diet, anyway."

Dylan said, "It's kinda like *The Breakfast Club* meets *Dog Day Afternoon,* isn't it?"

The group gave a cautious laugh. Even Bobby appeared to chuckle.

Alden gave Dylan a look of surprise.

Dylan shrugged. "I like old movies."

Carl looked down at his cell phone and huffed.

"What is it?" asked Jamie.

Carl turned the face of his phone toward Jamie. "No signal."

Jamie pulled his phone from his back pocket. "Mine too."

"Bobby?" Carl shouted, as he wobbled his phone in the air.

Bobby pulled his phone out and gave it a look. He shook his head.

"Jamie," said Carl. "Go check the water."

Jamie walked over to the counter, put a cup under the spigot, and pressed the lever. The water flowed freely.

"Water's good."

Carl yelled, "Bonehead! That's the water cooler!"

The five-gallon bottle gurgled loudly as more water flowed into the tank below.

"Go check the bathroom!"

"Oh, right. Okay." Jamie left the room.

Carl murmured, through almost clinched teeth. "Calling that boy an idiot would be giving him a promotion."

Carl and Jamie were cousins who'd grown up together in New Waverly. Jamie, 10 years Carl's junior, left home at 16, and moved in with Carl and his wife near Conroe.

Three years later, Carl filed for bankruptcy, and his wife filed for divorce.

Though Jamie moved out on his 24th birthday, he still looked for Carl's approval on most decisions—which almost never came.

Jamie returned. "No water in the bathroom."

Before Carl could reply, the phone on the branch manager's desk rang.

Jamie and Carl locked at each other. Neither moved.

Outside, they saw four vehicles now: three sedans and one van—clearly labeled Washington County SWAT.

To the relief of both men, after 10 rings, the sound stopped.

Five seconds later, it rang again.

Carl walked over to the desk, took a breath, and lifted the receiver.

Gabrielle listened for a moment. She heard only silence on the other end of the line.

She looked at Kooper and pointed to her ear.

Kooper tapped his surveillance headset and nodded. He mouthed, *he's there.*

"This is Gabrielle Layton with the Washington County Sheriff's office, and I'm here to talk with you. Who am I speaking with?"

Carl remained quiet.

"Look," she said. "Whoever you are, you can relax. The SWAT commander isn't planning to storm the place, and they're giving me time to see if you and I can fix this. We want everyone to end this day safely, including you."

When she spoke with hostage takers, Gabrielle always kept it hidden that she was both the negotiator and the SWAT team commander. It helped build the relationship. Doing so brought her to more of an eye-to-eye level with the person on the other end. That wouldn't happen if they knew she was also the boss.

Plus, if she needed to reject a demand or steer the conversation in a specific direction, she could blame it all on "The Boss," and still keep the lines of communication open.

The result? She could play both roles in a good cop–bad cop real-life police drama.

She said, "It's okay to talk to me."

"Okay, I'll listen. But no names," said Carl.

"Fair enough," said Gabrielle. "First things first. Everybody okay in there? Any of your crew, or the people in the bank, hurt?"

"Everyone's fine . . . for now. They'll stay that way unless you force me to make other arrangements."

"Thanks. I'll do my best to keep you from making that choice. But I gotta tell you something. If you start hurting people—the commander takes over. Decisions are taken outta my hands. You'll have to deal with a different group of officers who won't hesitate to end this in a much less pleasant way. So, let's make sure that you and I don't let that happen."

"Alright," said Carl. "But don't push it."

"Copy that."

Carl said nothing.

"Let me throw something out to you," said Gabrielle. "Is there anything we could do to end this peacefully now? Would you wanna just come on out and stop this before anything unintended happens and . . ."

Carl smirked. "Oh . . . sure, mind moving your people outta here first? We could grab the cash and leave." His voice intensified. "Then we could all wrap up the workday and go home early! Everybody wins!"

Gabrielle laughed a little. "No. No, we can't do that."

"Didn't think you would. So . . . no!"

Gabrielle looked over at Kooper and raised her brows. She pointed two fingers at her eyes, then one toward his laptop.

He gave her a thumbs-up.

"Okay," said Gabrielle, as she walked closer to the laptop and squinted to see the security feed. "Is there anything you need in there? Are you hungry? Did y'all have breakfast before you went to work this morning?"

Carl smiled like a graphic-novel villain. "Aww. How sweet. Thanks for asking. Yes. We ate."

He snarled in silence, then said, "We always eat and have a staff meeting before every bank robbery!"

"So you've done this before?"

Carl remained silent.

"You still with me?"

Finally, Carl replied, "Oh, there is one thing you could do for me."

"What's that?"

"Turn the water and phones back on. The hostages need to go to the bathroom, and I need to make a call."

Gabrielle frowned. *That term just won't do. We gotta do better than that.*

"Hey now," she said gently. "Let's not call them hostages. They're people, just like you and me. They've got families to feed . . . bills to pay . . . kids to get through school. They're no threat to you . . ."

"You think I care?"

After a moment, Gabrielle said, "Plus, that word, 'hostage,' gets Command a little jumpy."

She listened for a reply that never came.

Gabrielle said, "Anyway, you don't need the water and phones. You've got plenty of water in the cooler. And there's a phone in your hand, now. Anytime you pick it up—it automatically calls me."

"How'd you know we have plenty of water in the cooler?" asked Carl.

Gabrielle bent closer to Kooper's laptop. "Oh, it's a requirement in all banks. Standard operating procedure."

Five minutes earlier, SWAT established a direct feed into the bank's security cameras. Gabrielle could see the lobby from six different angles—a little detail she would keep between her and Kooper.

But dropping hints along the way? She loved the game. The perps would sense she was a step ahead. If they figured out how, they might disable the cameras—at least those they could see. If not, perhaps thinking SWAT already knew things could prove helpful.

Carl said, "If I think of anything, I'll let you know."

He slammed the phone down.

Hearing the noise, Bobby peeked out into the lobby. His stomach churned.

Carl, stay calm. If you make me choose—you lose.

"If you have enough money to support the life you want, and enough free time to enjoy using the money you have, in my opinion, you really are wealthy. And with that comes the independence and freedom."

—Alden Beckett

CHAPTER 4

A Victimless Crime?

10:15 a.m.

Cordelia looked at Alden. Her tears were gone, but her fear remained.

"Why are they doing this?"

Dylan chuckled. "I'll tell you why! I understand it. They're just gettin' their share. I've thought about doing the same thing. I don't do it—'cause I don't want to go to jail. But if I knew I wouldn't get caught . . . let's just say I wouldn't feel bad. The government insures banks anyway. It's basically a victimless crime. They're just stickin' it to the man!"

Bobby sighed and shook his head slightly. *Kid, you've got no clue what a bad idea this was.*

"That's actually not true," said Eddie. "The government insures customers against bank *failures*—not losses like these. We have to get an additional insurance policy to cover losses by events, like weather, or . . ."

"Or like robberies?" said Ayisha.

Eyes on Bobby, Eddie nodded.

Ayisha looked at Dylan. "Victimless crime? Not hardly. When any business's expenses rise—like their insurance premiums or taxes—they have to raise their prices and pass those costs along to us, if they want to stay in business. So, make no mistake," she nodded toward Bobby, "*we* are the victims of their so-called victimless crime. If they're stickin' it to the man, guess what, Dylan? *You* are that man."

She turned to Bobby. "No offense."

He said nothing. *None taken.*

Ayisha Holmes knew that point well. She'd moved to Brenham from Austin after receiving her medical degree and completing her residency. She now owned her private practice, specializing in dermatology.

"Well, maybe so, but I still get it," said Dylan. "They're just trying to get their slice of the pie. Money's scarce. They just want their fair share."

Alden said, "Dylan. Mind if I ask you something?"

Dylan leaned back and crossed his arms. "Sure. You seem to know pretty much everything else, anyway. Shoot."

Dylan quickly looked over at Bobby. "When I said shoot, I meant him. Not you." Looking back to Alden, he again said, "Shoot."

Bobby said nothing. But underneath his mask, he smirked. *This kid's funny.*

Alden thought the same.

"Help me understand your point of view," said Alden. "What makes it okay for them to rob the bank? And why do you think money is scarce?"

Dylan held up a finger. "First, I didn't say it was okay for them to rob the bank. I said I *understood* it, and I do. They're probably broke. Just . . . like . . . me. I've never made a lot of money. Nobody in my family ever did. Other people . . . those *rich* people . . . they got all the money. And they didn't leave much for folks like me. Don't matter how hard I work—which is much harder than they do—I can't get ahead."

Bobby raised his unseen brows. *Sounds familiar.*

Dylan said, "Why're you asking, Mr. Smart Guy? You some kinda money-man, or something?"

"Well, Dylan, that's actually Mr. Beckett's specialty," Eddie said.

Dylan looked at Alden. "What does he mean? *That's your specialty?*"

Alden was slow to answer.

"Let's just say I help people change their relationship with money. I teach them to see it through a different lens. Then I guide them to make smarter decisions that are in their best interest."

Eddie said, "Alden's helped me personally with my finances over the years. I've appreciated his help."

"What?" said Dylan. "You're a banker! You're supposed to know all that stuff already, right?"

"Well . . . I do know a lot. But Alden showed me I still had much to learn." Eddie chuckled, "You know, I'd never considered that even though I work with finances every day, I've had beliefs—unconscious beliefs—about money that were just . . . wrong. And they were limiting my potential to build a secure life for my family—robbing me of any chance at lasting wealth."

"Robbing you?" Dylan said, gesturing toward Bobby. "Kinda like that guy?"

Eddie sighed. "Yeah. Kinda like that guy."

"Not much difference," said Alden, as he looked around the room. "Hostages and robbers. Many people are victims—held hostage by their beliefs about money. And those beliefs are robbing their future. But when I help them change their perspective, they can change their actions and escape to a better life."

Dylan pursed his lips. "Okay, *Mr. Beckett,* since we have time on our hands, mind explaining those things to the rest of us? Or is that something you only share with bank presidents?"

"Bank managers," said Eddie, sounding almost embarrassed by his position.

How about bank robbers? Bobby dropped his eyes—definitely embarrassed by his.

Alden said, "Since you said I could call you Dylan, it's okay with me if you call me Alden. Fair enough?"

Dylan agreed.

"No," said Alden. "It's not something I only teach bank managers. I'm willing to share my insights with anyone who wants to learn. I even work with people professionally to help them make their financial future more secure."

Alden looked around the vault. "Yes, I think that would be a good idea. It may help us all keep our minds occupied in a good way."

The hostages sat up in their chairs, moved closer, and gathered in a semicircle around Alden, like strangers at a campfire who hoped to stay warm.

Alden looked up at Bobby. "Okay with you?"

Bobby nodded. *Where the heck were you last week?*

Alden tilted his head slightly. "Want to come in closer?"

Bobby looked back through the vault door and into the lobby. Carl and Jamie were busy making plans as to their next move. He leaned back against a table standing just a few feet away.

Looking back at Alden, he shook his head. *I need to keep an eye on Carl. It's probably too late for me, anyway.*

Bobby couldn't go back and prevent this day from happening. But if he could learn something from Alden, maybe his family's life would be much better down the road.

Gabrielle and Kooper watched the CCTV video in the SWAT Command van.

"How many feeds you get?" asked Gabrielle.

"Let's see . . . hmm . . . ATM, bank lobby, the convenience store across the street, and a traffic cam. We're looking at the ATM now."

The footage revealed three masked men entering the front doors.

Gabrielle looked outside through the bulletproof glass. "They came in from the south."

She pointed. "You have the footage from that convenience store?"

"Yes, ma'am. Coming right up."

The two stared at the laptop for several seconds.

"Stop," Gabrielle said.

From the edge of the screen, a car door shut, and a masked man appeared.

"Did he get out of that Chevy?" said Gabrielle.

"Hard to say. Let me pull up the traffic cam."

A few keystrokes later, they could see clearly.

"Yep. Running the plate now," said Kooper. "Let's see. Ah, yeah. Here it is. It's registered to a James Brown." In his best impression of the iconic music legend by the same name, he sang, "Wow! I feel good! Na-na-na-na-na-na-nut!"

Gabrielle shook her head and grimaced. "I wonder if that's how I sound when I sing in the shower."

Kooper laughed. "Everybody's a critic!"

He tapped on his keyboard. "Hang on a second. I'll check your apartment's CCTV footage. Wouldn't show your bathroom, but we may get some good audio."

Gabrielle raised an eyebrow. "You call it audio. The judge at your trial will call it evidence in a court of law."

Kooper smiled and quickly pulled his hands away from the keyboard. "Just kidding, boss. Just kidding."

Kooper glanced at his screen. "Hey, check this out. One of the cell phones in the bank is registered to a James Brown as well." Gabrielle picked up the SWAT line. "Let's see if the 'Godfather of Soul' is in the house."

The bank's phone rang again.

Carl pressed the speaker button. "Yes?"

"Hi James, this is Gabrielle. But please feel welcome to call me Gabi."

Gabrielle allowed almost no one to call her Gabi, except during hostage situations. She wanted the perps to feel a sense of familiarity with her.

"Nice try," said Carl. "But my name's not James."

Jamie, only catching the end of the statement, said, "What the . . . ?"

Carl quickly raised his hand. He brought his index finger to his lips and slowly shook his head.

Gabrielle sighed. *I wonder if they stole the car and phone, or if the name belongs to one of the other guys?*

She didn't belabor the point.

"Okay," she said. "My guys are gettin' a little hungry out here. I'm gonna order some food. Want me to get something for y'all as well? Maybe some pizzas?"

Carl hesitated. But Jamie, still silent, nodded quickly.

"Alright," said Carl. "Hey, why don't you have the delivery guy park at the front door. Tell him to walk away, but leave the engine running and the key in the ignition."

"What?" Gabrielle said. "You wanna leave? Lose the pleasure of my company already? I'm hurt."

Carl said, "Nothing personal."

"I'll run that idea by Command and see what I can do," said Gabrielle. "But don't get your hopes up."

"Same goes for your peaceful ending idea," said Carl.

Gabrielle said, "Hang in there. We'll figure this out. In the meantime, when the food gets here, I'll call back."

Carl disconnected the call.

Kooper grinned. "So, what did Command say?"

Gabrielle kept her eyes on the monitor. "She dismissed the idea. Didn't give it a second thought."

Carl said to Jamie, "Go check on the vault."

Jamie did as instructed.

After about 30 minutes, Gabrielle turned to Kooper.

"I've got an idea," she said. "But to make it work, we'll need to get all three men into the lobby. Those pizzas here yet?" she asked.

"Just arrived," said Kooper.

"Turn the bank manager's phone back on. We're gonna try something. It's a long shot . . . maybe we'll get lucky."

Kooper tapped a few quick keystrokes. "Done."

Gabrielle pulled out her cell phone, readied a text message, then used the SWAT line to call the lobby again.

Carl answered. "Yes."

"Hi. Gabi here again."

Carl sighed. "You certainly are."

Kooper fought his urge to laugh. *Poor guy.*

Gabrielle shot him a glance, and just like that, the urge went away.

"Command nixed the idea of the delivery driver," she said. "But the pizzas are here, and we need to get them to you."

Carl stayed quiet.

"What would you think about me having one of my people bring them to the front door? Maybe you could send one of your guys out to get it . . ."

"And let you grab him? I don't think so."

"That really wasn't my plan." Gabrielle said, "I want to get you and everyone else out safely."

She paused. "How about this? My guy drops them off at the door and walks away. You send one guy out to get them, while the other two of you stand guard."

Carl said nothing.

Finally, Gabrielle laughed. "Look, if we try anything, I'll send my guy back, and you can keep him. Alright?"

Kooper raised his brows. Gabrielle lowered hers.

She shook her head, and silently mouthed, *Just kidding.*

Carl reluctantly agreed. He summoned Jamie and Bobby from the vault.

As soon as Gabrielle saw all three men gathered near the lobby entrance, she looked at her cell phone and pressed send. The message was delivered.

Alden started to speak, but a soft buzz in the vault interrupted him.

Eddie leaned forward and peered out into the lobby. With caution, he retrieved his phone from his jacket pocket.

In the flurry of earlier activities, the robbers had overlooked the fact that there were seven people in the lobby—but they had only collected six cell phones.

Alden looked surprised.

"I palmed it," Eddie whispered. He looked at the screen and read a text message from a number he didn't recognize.

He handed the phone to Alden.

Alden read the text and grinned.

> **This is SWAT. Give the phone to the guy in the wheelchair.**

Alden tapped a quick reply.

They heard steps coming to the vault again: Bobby coming back with the pizza. Eddie looked at Alden, alarmed. *Bobby!* he mouthed soundlessly.

An instant before Bobby rounded the corner and came into the vault, Alden hit Send and jammed the phone underneath his leg.

"Money isn't a scarce resource even when it may feel like it. Money is abundant and will flow to value, creativity, and purpose."

—Alden Beckett

CHAPTER 5

Into the River of Money

11:00 a.m.

Gabrielle looked down at her phone and read Alden's message.

> 3 armed amateurs
> Guns—unloaded I think, except for guard's revolver
> Carl, Jamie and Bobby
> Carl is leader—has guard's gun
> Gabi?
> Gotta go

She replied to the text and hit the send button.

Bobby sat two pizzas on the table in the vault, then returned to the entrance, standing guard. Each captive took a slice.

As the others settled in, Alden got underway.

"Your beliefs about money will hold you hostage or set you free—the choice is yours. But with a productive money mindset and a few straightforward strategies, you can escape from financial bondage to financial independence."

"How can our beliefs affect our money?" asked Dylan. He clenched his eyes, tensed his fists, and said, "I can believe really hard that I'm rich." He opened his eyes and laughed. "But my bank account ain't fooled. It thinks I took a vow of poverty."

Bobby sighed. *Class clown.*

"Not what I meant," said Alden. "That's more of a wish."

Dylan said, "So, what *do* you mean?"

"Our beliefs," Alden said, "though often hidden, are behind the scenes—telling us what to do. They either throw roadblocks in our way or clear a path to freedom. They shape our economic destiny and affect how we earn and manage our daily cash flow. Our beliefs, right or wrong, impact our ability to build lasting wealth."

"So, what beliefs should we have?" asked Cordelia.

"Great question," said Alden. "I encourage my clients to embrace seven money truths that are the keys to unlocking financial independence."

Eddie pulled a pen from his coat pocket. "Hold on. I'm going to take notes." He wrote on the lid of one of the pizza boxes: Alden's Seven Money Truths.

Bobby smirked. *Teacher's pet.*

"The first truth sets the foundation for all the rest," Alden said.

1. We are responsible for our money beliefs and actions—choose wisely.

"Our journey to building wealth and financial independence begins with accepting that we alone are responsible for our beliefs and our fiscal condition," Alden said. "Even when outside events caused our present economic problems, *we* have to take the actions that will change our future. No one else can do that for us."

"Not fair!" Dylan said, "I've had a bunch of things outta my control cost me lots of money."

Bobby nodded. *I get it, kid. That's why I'm in this mess.*

Cacey said, "My husband lost his job when the company went out of business. Within a month, we were struggling to even buy food."

Alden nodded. "I understand."

He patted the arms of his wheelchair. "I'm not saying you are responsible for everything that happens to you. But you *are* responsible for how you respond to it—how you move forward from that point."

"Sounds like a little tough-love to me," said Dylan.

"Maybe so," said Alden. "But it's real.

"I had absolutely no control over what put me in this chair. But I had to accept responsibility for my future, anyway. If I'd waved the white flag, blamed the event, and given up—I would be in a very different situation now."

Bobby turned away. *Hard to argue with a man in a wheelchair. Can't exactly hit him with, "That's easy for you to say, buddy."*

"The journey of getting our finances in order starts between our ears," said Alden. "Changing our circumstances requires accepting ownership of our personal beliefs and actions.

"Can we all agree on that?"

Through some minor resistance, the group agreed.

Jamie walked into the vault and stood by Bobby.

He whispered, "What'd I miss?"

Bobby remained silent. *My guess . . . most of high school?*

"What are your beliefs about money?" Alden asked, "If I said, 'Fill in the blank: money is . . . what?' What would your answer be?"

Dylan didn't hesitate. "Scarce. I'm always out."

"The cause of marital problems," said Cordelia.

Bobby gave a stealth nod.

Eddie said, "Never discussed. But hoarded at home for hard times."

"Why rich people are better than me," said Yen.

"I've got one," Ayisha said. "Can't buy you happiness."

Cordelia laughed. "That was my grandma's favorite. That, and money is the root of all evil."

"*I'll* tell you what money is," said Dylan. "It's the thing that turns all those rich people into greedy, dishonest, lying, cheating bast . . ."

Alden held up his hand. "We get the point, Dylan."

Cacey blushed and half-raised her hand. "Money is cold and hard. You know, like cold, hard, cash?"

Alden laughed. "Whoever told you that lied to you."

"They did?"

"Yes, ma'am. Cash isn't cold or hard."

"It's not?"

Giving himself a snuggle, Alden said, "No. It's warm . . . and cuddly. Makes you feel safe and secure."

Everyone laughed.

Alden said, "Our beliefs about money are often not based in fact. And I'll come back to each of those you mentioned."

"Dylan, let's begin with what you said earlier—scarce," said Alden.

The young man took a bite of pepperoni. "Alright. Knock yourself out."

Alden looked around the room. "A scarcity mindset . . . thinking that there isn't much money out there, will block your ability to build wealth."

"What wealth?" said Dylan. "How exactly am I *supposed* to think about money . . . when I don't have none?"

Bobby understood. *Ditto. But the phrase is, "I don't have any."*

"I get it," Alden said. "Before I learned these truths about money, I was broke myself. I lived paycheck to paycheck . . ."

"Been there. Done that," said Dylan. "Couldn't afford the T-shirt."

Alden smiled. "Do you remember when you first learned to believe money was in limited supply, if I may ask?"

"Sure do," said Dylan. "It was from my dad. He was a good man. Worked hard all his life—45 years with the same company. Never got ahead. Died broke."

Dylan shook his head and sighed. "Wanna know what his favorite saying was?"

"Sure," said Alden.

"Anytime I would ask for anything, he'd say, 'I'm sorry, son. There's just not enough money.'"

Alden nodded, then looked down.

"Dylan. I'm a dad too." He lifted his eyes. "And though I've never had the pleasure of meeting yours, I can promise you something."

"What?"

"That was *not* his favorite saying. It probably broke his heart every time the words trickled over his lips."

Dylan said nothing but felt the salty sting of tears.

Bobby did too.

Alden said, "That brings us to the second truth about money."

2. Money isn't scarce, even when it feels like it.

Bobby considered coughing and calling, "BS," under his breath.

Dylan beat him to the punch.

"I'll explain," said Alden.

He reached for one of the pizza boxes.

"Most people think of money like this pizza—a limited commodity. Scarce." Counting, he said, "There are what—eight slices there? Once someone eats a slice, it's gone. There's no further benefit to anyone."

Dylan said, "That's the American Dream—get your slice of the pie!"

"You certainly hear that a lot," Alden said. "But it's wrong."

Dylan smirked. "I wouldn't know."

"The money supply isn't like a pie—a limited resource. Instead, it flows, similar to the currents created as the sun warms the Earth's atmosphere. That movement spawns opportunities, fosters growth, and enriches lives around the world. When money gets into circulation, we, and countless others, benefit. Like air—breathing in and out—it's an abundant life force that connects us all."

Dylan laughed. "Money's a life force? May the force be with me, baby!"

Bobby stifled a chuckle. *That boy ain't right.*

"How is money a life force that connects us all?" asked Cordelia.

Eddie raised his finger. "One way is how money changes hands when we buy things. I found a website that tracked the journey of a $100 bill. They printed their web address on the back of the bill, and asked people to go online and tell where they were, and what they purchased with it."

"That's interesting," said Alden. "Do you remember how many times it changed hands?"

"No," replied Eddie. "But it accounted for over a million dollars' worth of transactions. A single $100 bill, and thousands of people, literally worldwide, benefited."

"That's a lot of spending, huh?" Alden said.

Cordelia laughed. "I'm good at that part . . . the spending part. I really, *really*, like that part."

"Putting money into savings and investment accounts," said Alden, "is also a vital part of the process."

"Pfft," said Dylan. "Interest rates aren't so great sometimes. How does that help us that much—or the world, for that matter?"

"Wanna take this one, Eddie?" Alden asked, "What happens to the money deposited into savings or investment accounts?"

Eddie acknowledged the current interest rates. "Well, when interest rates are low, it's true that the money you earn isn't much.

"However, the real magic happens because your money doesn't just sit here. We get you into that circulation by loaning your money to others. We make business loans, car loans, mortgages, and personal loans."

"That's local," said Ayisha. "How does that have any global impact?"

Eddie smiled. "Let me tell you about one of our business customers in the area.

"We loaned her money to start a bakery. She bought equipment, supplies, and opened up shop. People loved her goods so much, she quickly expanded and hired employees. Those workers now spread the money she pays them throughout our local economy, on food, rent, and raising their families. Many businesses benefit."

"You're talking about Mother Mabel's, aren't you?" Ayisha said.

Eddie nodded. "Normally, I couldn't disclose that information. But Mother Mabel's story is so impressive, I asked for permission to share the details. She agreed."

Ayisha smiled as she took in a slow, deep breath. "Her croissants are delicious."

"One day," said Eddie, "a gentleman from London came in and bought some pastries. He loved them. Eventually, he negotiated the rights to manufacture and distribute her products in Europe. So now, employees, suppliers, and many others around the world are experiencing the same benefit as we do locally."

"The local news interviewed her," said Ayisha. "Such a great story."

"When you invest," Eddie said, "it works similarly. Investing is really just a more sophisticated form of saving. There's simply a little more risk."

Alden said. "When we put our money into savings and investments, we're breathing out. When we earn a nice return, we're breathing in. And this process helps an uncountable number of of people around the world."

Eddie nodded. "We just have to tap into that flow."

"So, why does believing money is scarce even matter?" Ayisha asked. "What's the difference?"

"We humans have survival instincts," said Alden. "They've been engrained into us for generations. When we think we may not have enough money for food or other basic needs, our brain's neurological system kicks in. We go into a scarcity mindset.

"Our amygdala . . ."

"Our what?" Dylan asked.

"Our amygdala—the part of our brain that generates emotions of all types—positive and negative."

"Oh. *That* amygdala," said Dylan. He nodded. "Yeah. I knew that. Go ahead . . . tell 'em about it."

Alden smiled. "When we're in a scarcity mindset, our amygdala generates fear-based emotions—the fear of not having enough to survive. Our brain automatically shoots an electric charge down into our torso—producing a somatic marker. We literally feel something different, physiologically."

"Like butterflies in your stomach?" asked Cacey.

Bobby silently agreed. *More like buzzards for me.*

Alden nodded. "Exactly. A sense of uneasiness creeps in. And we don't like that feeling."

"Makes me feel pissed-off," said Dylan.

Cordelia laughed.

Alden said, "This scarcity mindset causes our fluid intelligence to nosedive. It stifles our ability to reason, analyze, and adapt to new circumstances. Making wise decisions gets much more difficult. We go into a protective, loss-aversion mentality."

"Makes sense, doesn't it?" said Ayisha. "You have to protect your own."

"We are indeed pre-wired for exactly that," Alden agreed. "But it can make us become needy, or greedy, or a combination of both."

"Like those rich people my dad worked for," Dylan said.

Alden replied, "Maybe. Maybe not. Greed and financial despair are actually two sides of the same scarcity mindset coin.

The belief that money is scarce leads some people to mentally justify their unacceptable actions. They're willing to do anything to survive."

Alden looked at Bobby and Jamie. "No offense, guys. But a scarcity mindset is likely what led you three here today. Your survival instincts combined with a sense of hopelessness, and you decided it was alright to take someone else's money—something that's clearly wrong."

Dylan asked, "Are you defending those greedy corporations?"

"No. But, Dylan, corporations aren't greedy."

"The hell they aren't!"

Alden smiled and raised his hand. "Wait. Let me explain."

Dylan crossed his arms and leaned back in his chair.

"If you get drunk," said Alden, "then climb behind the steering wheel of your car and hurt somebody . . . is your car at fault? Or are you?"

"Me," Dylan said, "I'm the driver."

Alden nodded. "That's right. When a car is driven by an intoxicated person, it's a danger to society.

"A corporation is just a thing . . . like your car. And when a corporation is being 'driven' by a greedy person, it's not so great for society either."

Dylan said nothing.

"Most people choose not to get behind the wheel after drinking," said Alden. "And most corporations are run by honest people who try to do the right thing. Their goal is to generate income by providing value to their customers. Then, they pay their expenses, including their employees, and earn a profit. The more people they serve—the greater profit they make."

"My husband's boss was greedy," Cacey said. "It all came out after they closed down."

Alden empathized. "I'm sorry you went through that. But my experience tells me that's the exception—not the rule."

Alden looked around the room. "What about you all? If you ran the largest corporation in the world, would you still try to do the right thing on a daily basis? You'd treat people fairly, right?"

Everyone nodded . . including Dylan . . . eventually.

"Whether you're wealthy or financially strapped, a scarcity mindset puts pressure on you to make bad choices. Greed can show its gnarly face regardless of your bank balance."

Alden scanned the room. "That brings us to the third money truth."

3. Money flows like a river—jump in.

Alden posed a question to the group. "How much water do you think's in the Colorado River?"

Cacey grinned. "A lot."

"A *boat*load?" Dylan said, proud of his pun.

Alden smiled. "It's helpful to think of money like water in a river—constantly moving. There's over $17 trillion in cash and bank accounts circulating in the United States alone. And that doesn't even include other non-cash investments, such as mutual funds, bonds, and real estate."

Dylan piped up again. "That's a *ship*load!" His double entendre failed to impress his silent and captive audience.

"That's right," said Alden. "$17 trillion is a *ship*load of money."

Dylan felt vindicated.

Alden said, "The cycle of water keeps rivers flowing. We get rain. It flows along into streams and rivers and eventually reaches the oceans. Some sinks into the water table, benefiting people, plants, and animals. Some evaporates into the clouds, and returns with the next shower, starting the process all over again. Each step in that cycle feeds the next."

Dylan laughed. "You sound like my high school science teacher, Mr. Hinson. Maybe I should've paid more attention."

Alden smiled. "Maybe so."

Bobby remembered Mr. Hinson too. *He was my favorite teacher.*

Alden said, "The total amount of water within the cycle stays pretty much the same. But the benefit to everyone happens because the cycle keeps repeating."

"So, what does that mean to us?" Ayisha asked.

Alden tilted and raised a brow. "Money may move like a river. But to take advantage, you have to jump in and get into the flow. If you sit on the bank, watching and wishing you could join the fun, but never actually take the plunge . . . you're a spectator, and not going very far."

Cacey looked down. "Apparently, my husband and I aren't very good swimmers."

Alden smiled at Cacey. "Swimming's not your only option. There are inner tubes and canoes. You can even speed along in a boat. Faster ways are available. You just need to know where to seek help and decide to jump in."

Dylan laughed. "I'd jump in my canoe, but it's up scat creek without a paddle."

Alden shook his head and grinned. "Changing from a scarcity mindset to an abundance mindset, and getting into the flow of money by investing, will help you get your canoe unstuck. It still requires work. But you can get where you want to go much sooner."

Carl walked into the vault. "How's it going in here?"

"Fine," said Bobby, uttering his first word that anyone in the vault could hear.

He immediately realized his mistake.

Son of a . . .

No one seemed to give it much thought.

Well . . . almost no one.

Unlock THE VAULT
Secure the combination to access your FREE Resources

Visit **www.HiddenHeistVault.com** to claim your exclusive access to The Vault - a treasure trove of complimentary guides and insights.

If you experience any difficulty registering for The Vault, please email **support@referralcoach.com**

ALDEN'S SEVEN MONEY TRUTHS

1. We are responsible for our money beliefs and actions — choose wisely.
2. Money isn't scarce, even when it feels like it.
3. Money flows like a river – jump in.

Abbondanza Pizza

CHAPTER 6

The Hidden Heist of False Perceptions

12:30 p.m.

One of the advances in modern law enforcement is how quickly technology can find information. Once Alden had given Gabrielle the names of Carl, Jamie, and Bobby, Kooper quickly cross-referenced them with the cell phones he had pinged earlier. He searched for rap sheets on all three but found only one.

He turned his laptop to Gabrielle. "Here ya go. That's everything we've got on Carl Grainger."

Gabrielle leaned in. "Thirty-seven years old. Yada, yada, yada . . . looks like he has a relatively clean record."

"Yep," said Kooper "Minor stuff. Traffic tickets, mostly."

Gabrielle's finger scrolled down the screen—then came to a dead stop.

"What have we here?" Gabrielle said. "Got weird four years ago . . . two drunk and disorderly charges, a car repossessed, and an assault complaint from a bar fight."

Kooper entered a few more keystrokes. "Assault complaint was dropped. Says here that the bar's security footage clearly showed that Carl dodged another man's punch before returning the favor with a quick right hook."

"Can you pull up anything that tells us what happened to him around that time?" Gabrielle asked. "Something changed."

With a few more keystrokes, Kooper accessed court records. "Filed for bankruptcy and got divorced four and a half years ago."

Gabrielle sighed. "Hmm."

Carl walked slowly back from the vault to the lobby desk. Jamie followed.

The bank's phone rang again.

Carl's mind raced. *What the heck do I do now? Make demands? Wait and see what SWAT does? I never wanted hostages.*

He was supposedly in control but felt like a hostage himself. And when the phone rang, it gave him the same gut-rumble as when bill collectors called. It made him nauseous.

Jamie got to the phone before Carl and hit the speaker button. "Community Savings and Loan. How may I direct your call?"

Gabrielle laughed. "I like that! A sense of humor is a good way to release tension. That's helping us both . . . uh . . . who is this? What should I call *you*?"

Before Jamie could reply, Carl moved him to the side. "Nice try."

Gabrielle laughed. "Your admin's got a friendly voice. What's his name?"

"Remind me to give him a raise," said Carl. "You don't need his name. But you can call *me* boss."

"Oh, boss is too formal," said Gabrielle. "I'll pick a name for you."

She paused. "Hmm. Let me think . . . how about Carl?"

Carl froze.

"Is everything still alright in there?"

No reply.

"You still with me, Carl?"

"For now."

Gabrielle said, "Since we aren't going anywhere for a while, mind if I ask you a couple of questions, just to get to know you a bit?"

"Mind if I ask *you* a question?"

"Sure, go ahead."

"Why Carl?"

"That's my father's middle name. Why?" She laughed. "Did I get it right?"

Carl said nothing.

"Wow! I got that right, didn't I? Hey, Carl, that's a good thing. Maybe it's a sign that we'll figure this out, so nobody gets hurt. That's a big win!"

Carl said, "Don't count your chickens just yet."

Gabrielle looked at the laptop screen and tapped Kooper's shoulder. She mouthed, *I need to see his face,* as she made the pinch-to-zoom gesture.

Kooper enlarged the frame. Carl's face was completely obscured by his disguise. She could see nothing.

Gabrielle said, "So, have you given any thought about how you'd like to come out of this? How do you and I create a happy ending here?"

"Not sure there can be one," said Carl. "Your commander said no before. Do I need to hurt somebody to get his cooperation?"

Gabrielle smirked. *Why do they always assume it's a man?*

"No threats, Carl. Okay? Don't lose faith. As long as you're not harming people, we can help each other. I'm not sure how to resolve this safely yet either. But I'm 100 percent sure that you and I are the two best people to figure that out. We'll make it work."

Carl said nothing. He disconnected the call.

Carl believed one thing was certain. The longer this went on, the more likely something would go terribly wrong.

He was bluffing Gabrielle. He wanted to escape with the money—but he didn't want anyone to get hurt. Least of all, himself.

He'd endured enough hurt for one lifetime.

In the vault, everyone finished their pizza. Eddie closed the second box with the remaining few slices, saving every bite of leftovers.

Alden started back up. "So, let's keep going . . . "

"No! Let's not," said Ayisha. "What's going on out there? I want out of here."

"Me too," said Dylan, standing.

Bobby said nothing but moved directly into the open vault door and crossed his arms.

Kid, don't do this.

Alden said, "Sit back down, Dylan."

"Why?"

"These situations take time."

Alden looked at Bobby, then back to Dylan, and smiled.

"Plus, you'd be boxing way out of your weight class."

"Oh, I don't know," said Dylan. "Maybe we can double-team him. I'll hit him high—you roll in low."

Dylan slowly returned to his seat. "Sorry if that was tacky. No offense intended. But you look tough enough to me."

Alden smiled. "None taken. I am pretty solid. And the chair has some serious cross-bracing. But that's a *really* bad idea. We don't want to do things in here that make it worse out there." He scanned the faces in the vault. "Let's all stay calm."

As the pressure subsided, Alden asked, "Okay to keep going?"

The group reluctantly agreed.

Alden looked at Ayisha. She consented as well.

"What do you all remember about your parents and their relationship with money?" Alden said, "What'd they think?"

Dylan smirked. "My parents' relationship with money was like a bad country song."

"What do you mean?" asked Yen.

With a distinctive nasal twang, reminiscent of the Grand Ole Opry stars of the mid-20th century, Dylan sang.

> *She ran off, left no note,*
> *She didn't think I'm funny.*
> *The kids need shoes, the electric's off,*
> *And there's no milk or honey.*
>
> *Who's this girl that left you,*
> *For some place bright and sunny?*
> *Wasn't Reba, Wynette, or Tammy,*
> *Instead, her name was money.*

Ayisha laughed. "Dylan. That was . . . uh . . . painful."

The others chimed in as well, each giving Dylan their own critique. To his credit, he took it all in stride.

"So . . . you're all saying I should keep my day job at the car repair center?"

"Yes!" the group replied in unison.

Alden raised his brows at Dylan. "Tough crowd."

"Seriously," said Alden to the group. "Tell me what you remember about your parents and their discussions about finances."

"My folks don't talk about money—they fight about it," said Cordelia. "When they don't have enough, they argue about needing more. When they have plenty, they can't agree how to spend it. It's a constant battle. My dad yells . . . says Mom's calling him a failure. Says she's always nagging him about money."

"How do you react?" Alden asked.

Cordelia looked down and sighed.

"Truthfully? It scares me. Their arguments can be intense. Makes me anxious. I was glad to get a place of my own—just wanted to get away from it. Money's the cause."

"When you think about your personal money situation now," Alden said, "how does it make you feel?"

"Much the same as when they fight. I get nervous. Don't want to talk about it. I usually bury my head in the sand like an ostrich and hide from anything to do with money."

Eddie said, "It's funny you asked about our parents. As I gathered the pizza scraps and put them back into the box, I could almost hear my mother's voice."

"What was she saying?" asked Alden.

"She was telling me not to waste any food. Gather it all up and save it for hard times . . ."

Eddie's sentence may have trailed off, but Alden read his expression.

"Go on," said Alden.

"My parents grew up in troublesome times. And their parents grew up in the Great Depression of the 1930s. Jobs were lacking. Despair was plentiful. They didn't have much and were afraid of losing what little they had. The stock market scared them. Banks weren't to be trusted. They literally kept their cash in a coffee can above the refrigerator."

Jamie walked back into the vault as Eddie finished his comment. He said, "In a coffee can? Uh, could I get an address on that? Bobby, you got anything to write on?"

Bobby didn't move. *Moron!*

Eddie looked at Cordelia. "My folks didn't fight about money. But there were definitely some unspoken rules about the subject. The main one being you didn't discuss money in polite company. I couldn't imagine myself ever asking my dad how much money he made."

"Same here," said Yen. "About the only time I remember my parents having any conversation around the subject was when they would talk about wealthy people. They held them in such high esteem. We treated everyone we met with respect. That's just how my parents raised me. But the way they talked about rich people—was different."

"What do you mean?" asked Dylan.

Yen got quiet. "There was almost a reverence in their voice, as if they were talking about people who were better than us. As I got older, I understood that the respect my parents showed was about the accomplishments of the people, rather than the money they had. But for me, I grew up thinking that I wasn't as good as the wealthy."

"Same here," said Ayisha.

Alden nodded. "I understand. For a while, in my early 20s, I was in sales. I wasn't very good. Yet, I had colleagues who were excellent. They made lots of money. They owned large houses, nice cars, and stylish clothes."

He shook his head and sighed.

"I used to really talk bad about them. I would tell my friends how *those* people were so materialistic. All they cared about was money. And I would never want to be like them."

Bobby could relate. *Said the same about the managers on my last job.*

Alden said, "The problem wasn't them, though. It was me. They never acted better than me or boasted about their accomplishments. But every time I saw their successes, I also saw my failures. They weren't rubbing their achievements in my face—I was. My lack of performance poured salt into the open wounds of my ego. I guess I thought by putting them down, I was raising myself up, at least in the eyes of my friends."

The vault was quiet.

Eddie broke the silence. "That reminds me of the messages we get every day from movies, television, and our culture." Looking around, he asked, "When's the last time you saw a rich man in a movie—who was actually portrayed as the good guy? It seems like Hollywood's intentionally saying that anyone who's rich is dishonest, greedy, or . . ."

"Or a banker?" Dylan said with a smirk.

Everyone laughed.

"Just kidding," said Dylan.

Eddie nodded. "I get it. It's kind of funny. Funny, until you're the one they're portraying that way. Especially when you know it's not true. At least not in your case."

Alden said, "That brings us to our fourth truth about money."

4. Childhood and cultural money messages mislead us—challenge them.

"Messages we've repeatedly heard, whether from our parents, our culture, or the entertainment industry, work their way into our subconscious. Without thinking about them or challenging the premise, we internalize those undertones and act accordingly. The result? Those incorrect cues cause us to choose some very unproductive behaviors."

Cacey spoke softly. "Like what?"

"Good question," Alden said.

She smiled.

Alden couldn't help it. He smiled too.

"When someone grows up internalizing messages that say you can't let go of anything, because you may not have enough later . . . or that you can't trust banks, investments, or the stock market . . . it can be difficult for them to put their cash into places where their money works for them."

"I'll attest to that," said Eddie as he raised his hand. "I've had a fear that I may lose everything and not have enough money for my wife and me to live out our years."

"That mistaken way of thinking," said Alden, "can cause people to miss out completely on what has historically been a nice return on investments."

Eddie smiled. "I'm doing better. But I'm still a work in progress."

"Don't feel bad," Alden said. "The wiring of our brain compounds this effect. We're psychologically inclined to be averse to loss. Our natural emotional response to potentially losing something is much stronger than our response to possible gain. It's ingrained in our DNA. But an excellent financial advisor can help you manage those fears and develop an overall plan based on the risk tolerance you have."

"Mine did," said Eddie, acknowledging Alden's help.

Alden looked at Cordelia. "If arguments about money were predominant in your youth, your tendency will be to have those same spats in your own relationships. Or you may simply refuse to have financial discussions at all, just to avoid the potential conflict."

Cordelia nodded. "That would be me."

Bobby sighed. *Me too.* He remembered the gut-punch he felt every time his wife wanted to discuss their finances—and how he always walked away.

"If you think rich people are better than you," Alden said, "your plans to build your own wealth may get derailed by your self-image. You'll think you're not deserving. And if you think all people who've done well financially are greedy crooks—each time you set goals to create your own abundance, you'll struggle. It creates a spiritual conflict."

Dylan raised his hand, tilted his head back. "Amen, brother Alden! Tell us more! Tell us more!"

Alden moved slightly away from Dylan and said, "Just in case we get lightning in the vault."

Dylan ducked and looked skyward.

Everyone laughed.

"On one hand," said Alden, "you think you want to accumulate wealth. But on the other, you think wealthy people are bad. You'd be trying to become something that you secretly look down on. You'll never get comfortable with that idea."

"So, what's the answer?" asked Ayisha. "What do we do?"

Alden shook his head. "I wish there was a simple answer. But there's not. My best advice is to become aware. Take notice of how our mistaken beliefs about money get baked into us by societal messaging. Recognize them. Then *challenge* those beliefs."

Alden nodded to Dylan. "Are all rich people really dishonest? Of course not. Look at the donors of the greatest charities in the world and see where the money's coming from."

Carl walked in.

He tapped Bobby's arm. "We need to discuss some things."

The men left the vault.

Alden said, "Do all money discussions have to end in an argument? No. Are all investments so risky that you could lose everything? Not really. Historically, with sound financial advice, your returns from a variety of investments can be consistent over the long haul. One of my favorite quotes is, 'It's not *timing* the market that creates wealth . . . it's your time *in* the market.'"

"What does that mean?" Dylan asked.

"Have you ever heard anybody say they were waiting until the stock market was good before they'd invest their money? Or maybe when it dropped, they bailed out, thinking they would protect their cash for now, and get back in when things get better."

Cordelia nodded. "I have."

"They were trying to time the market," said Alden. "But since nobody can really predict the future, it doesn't work very well."

"Yeah, but what about that Warren Buffett guy?" Dylan asked. "He does pretty well."

Every head in the vault turned toward Dylan. There was complete silence.

Dylan looked around the room. "What? I can read."

Alden smiled. "I'm impressed, Dylan. But *that Warren Buffett guy* is one of the wealthiest people in the world. And he doesn't jump in when he thinks the timing's right. He's been investing for decades.

His strategy is to buy into companies that are undervalued and have sound financials—then he holds them for the long-term. That's the difference. Warren says, 'If you aren't thinking about owning a stock for 10 years, don't even think about owning it for 10 minutes.'"

"Ten years! Ten years ago, I was in the eighth grade," said Dylan.

Alden laughed. "Getting sound advice from a good financial advisor, and then staying in for the long haul, has historically proven to provide the best return."

Alden looked around at each person in the vault.

"If you forget everything else about this day . . ."

"That's not happening," said Dylan.

Alden nodded and smiled. "Just remember what I said at the beginning. Your beliefs about money will either hold you hostage or set you free—the choice is yours. These mistaken beliefs come from messages we've internalized for decades. Unless you intentionally change them, and the actions that result, they're robbing you of your financial future."

"Like a hidden heist?" asked Dylan.

"That's right, Dylan. Like a hidden heist."

With Bobby out of the vault, Alden checked a text message on Eddie's phone, which had vibrated just a few minutes earlier.

> Yeah, it's me.
> Are you ever going to call me Gabrielle?
> Thanks for the intel.
> Still working the problem from out here.
> Seeing any escalation in there?

Alden replied as Eddie added more notes to the pizza box.

> No. So far, so good.
> People in vault getting nervous.

Alden hit Send.
Gabrielle's reply buzzed back.

> Keep them calm.
> Last thing we need is for one of them to make these guys more nervous.

Carl, Jamie, and Bobby gathered around the branch manager's desk.

Carl said, "Boys, we can't stay in here much longer. We need a plan for how to get out of this situation. And shooting our way out is not an option."

"That's good," said Jamie. "My aim sucks! Plus, I only agreed because we said nobody would get hurt."

"Oh . . . that, and your gun isn't loaded," Bobby said.

Jamie laughed. "Oh yeah. And my gun isn't loaded."

Carl turned to Bobby. "You got any ideas?"

"No," he said.

At least none that you're gonna like, anyway.

ALDEN'S SEVEN MONEY TRUTHS

1. We are responsible for our money beliefs and actions — choose wisely.
2. Money isn't scarce, even when it feels like it.
3. Money flows like a river – jump in.
4. Childhood and cultural money messages mislead us — challenge them.

Abbondanza Pizza

CHAPTER 7

Secrets in the Vault

1:00 p.m.

Gabrielle and Kooper were discussing their strategy, when Kooper suddenly looked to the right side of the bank.

"What the heck? Who's that?"

Seeing what was happening, Gabrielle said, "Ring the lobby. Now!"

The phone rang as Carl, Jamie, and Bobby were still discussing their next steps.

Carl pressed the speakerphone button.

"What?"

"Carl, this is Gabi."

"Gabi who?"

"Cute. But no time for that right now."

Her tone was serious. However, there was no urgency in her voice. It was almost soothing.

"What's going on?" Carl asked.

"Carl, I need to tell you something."

The three men stared at the phone. Neither said a word. No one breathed.

"You still with me, Carl?"

"Yeah. What's happening?"

"I want you to know that we are *not* moving in on you."

"Okay," said Carl, intensity growing in his voice. "What *are* you doing?"

Gabrielle said, "About a minute ago, a deputy sheriff's car pulled up to the side of the bank. It's not one of ours. He's from Austin County."

Carl, Jamie, and Bobby immediately looked out the lobby's side windows. On the south side of the building, a uniformed deputy was ducking low and trying to make his way around the corner.

"I thought I could trust you, Gabi! I guess I was wrong!"

Gabrielle paused and looked at Kooper.

She took a slow breath. *Soothe him down.*

"Hey, I understand, Carl. But it's okay to stay calm. I have no idea what the guy's doing. But since Command didn't send him, he's not coming for you. I haven't lied to you yet. Not gonna start now. My job's to get you and everyone else out safely."

The deputy had seen the commotion at the bank and pulled over. Instead of going around the block and parking, he was trying to make his way over to the SWAT Command van on foot. A decision that could ruin the day and possibly end his career.

The three men in the lobby and the entire Washington County SWAT team watched as the deputy made a break from the corner of the building. He ran, full throttle, toward the van.

Though the winter storm passed through the night before, temperatures were above freezing by noon. Most of the wintry slush had melted into a patchwork of puddles. However, there was still a stretch of ice on the sidewalk, beneath the shade of a Bradford pear tree.

The deputy was heading straight for it.

He didn't see the ice until he was directly on top of it, and his pace caused him to slip. His arms flailed, a desperate attempt to maintain his balance.

At first, it appeared he would keep his footing. Unsteady, like a novice ice-skater, he skidded for three or four seconds. Then suddenly, his feet went into the air, and he hit the concrete pathway, hard.

He laid there, flat on his back, not moving a muscle.

Carl, Jamie, and Bobby, along with Gabrielle and Kooper, yelled in unison, "Whoa!"

"Ouch," said Kooper.

Jamie said, "That'll leave a mark!"

In order to add a little levity and defuse the tension of the moment, Gabrielle swiftly scribbled something on her notepad, stepped outside the van to make herself visible, and continued to hold the phone.

She held up the pad.

Like a judge's scorecard in an Olympic competition, it said, 7.5.

Jamie laughed. "Dang, Gabi! That's mean. I would have given him at least an eight."

"Maybe so," said Gabrielle. "But I penalized him for being an idiot."

Everyone sighed and laughed . . . even Carl.

"Carl, would it be alright if we come pick him up and bring him to the ambulance?"

"You really didn't send him?"

"No. And I don't know what the heck he was trying to accomplish. But I'll damn sure find out."

Carl agreed, and Gabrielle sent the EMTs to the sidewalk.

"Thanks, Carl. I appreciate you letting us do that. If you need anything, just pick up the phone. It'll dial me automatically."

She walked back into the van and looked at Kooper. "I get a sense that Carl's softening a bit."

The three robbers huddled.

"Jamie, go take a look out the back door and see if there's any way to escape," said Carl. "We need a way outta here."

Jamie departed.

"What do you have in mind?" Bobby asked.

"I'm not sure yet. We may have to take a hostage with us."

"And go where?" Bobby said. "You don't seriously think they'll just let us leave, do you?"

"Maybe," said Carl. "We could get them to charter us a plane to Mexico or something."

"Carl. There's no way they'll let us do that. Plus, I'm not leaving without my wife."

"You're married? Wait. Let me rephrase that. You're *that* married?" Carl said.

Bobby said, "Yes, Carl. I'm *that* married. I love my wife. I'm not leaving her behind."

Carl started to speak. But then he sighed and shook his head in disbelief.

Bobby shrugged. "Hey, not every marriage ends in a nuclear holocaust like yours did."

"Where do you live?" Carl said. "Is it close enough that we could swing by and get her?"

Bobby said nothing.

He'd only known Carl for a couple of months, and didn't want him anywhere near his wife or his home.

A mutual acquaintance—and old friend from high school, nicknamed Stoney—had introduced Bobby to Carl and Jamie. Bobby's wife never liked Stoney, and insisted he end their friendship a decade earlier.

Bobby tried to justify their friendship. "Look, I know Stoney has a less than stellar reputation, but . . ."

"Less than stellar?" Bobby's wife had said. "Neighborhood kids call him the *Reefer Wrangler*! Do you think he got the nickname Stoney by coincidence? He was always into things he shouldn't be doing. I'm sure he's growing pot and selling it now, and I don't want him around you or our family."

Bobby's wife was completely unaware he'd reconnected with Stoney.

Bobby had been out of work for months, and the couple was in serious financial trouble. He thought Stoney might help him find some kind of work—even if that meant he may have to inch his toe into the waters of illegality. But a bank robbery? That was much more than just a toe. He'd jumped into the deep end of the criminal lagoon and was now trying desperately not to drown.

Jamie returned from the back. "Can't go that way. Cops are there too."

"Okay," said Carl. Turning back to Bobby, he asked, "So, when we get out of here, can we go get your wife?"

Jamie laughed. "You're married?"

"Yes Jamie, I'm married."

Bobby looked back at Carl. "She's not home."

"How do you know that?" asked Carl.

Bobby looked down and sighed.

After a moment, his face lifted, and he looked at Carl—direct and unflinching. "Because she's the redhead in the vault."

Carl kicked a chair and moved nose-to-nose with Bobby. "She's WHAT?"

Unlock THE VAULT
Secure the **combination** to access your FREE Resources

Visit **www.HiddenHeistVault.com** to claim your exclusive access to The Vault - a treasure trove of complimentary guides and insights.

*If you experience any difficulty registering for The Vault, please email **support@referralcoach.com***

CHAPTER 8

Become Financially Literate

1:15 p.m.

"She's in the vault," Bobby repeated.

Carl couldn't believe what he was hearing. "What do you mean? Why is she here?"

Bobby sighed. "I'm not sure. This morning, she mentioned she was going out to apply for some jobs. She didn't say where. But when we came in, there she was . . . sitting in front of the bank manager."

Jamie laughed. "Dude! Did she know you were doing this?"

"No! Of course not! She would've pitched a fit!"

"So, we just happened to pick the bank where your wife was applying for a job?"

"Apparently so."

Jamie snorted. "Wow! It's a family business. She's applying for a bank job . . . and you're pulling one!"

Carl glared. "Shut up, Jamie! Let me think."

As Carl paced, Jamie sat down, and Bobby returned to the vault.

The vault was a custom-built room with a state-of-the-art locking system. The interior was well lit and made predominantly of stainless steel.

It certainly wasn't a cozy space. Instead, it was cold and sterile.

But the group of strangers who'd discovered themselves thrown into such a stressful day within the walls of their makeshift classroom were, in fact, warming to each other.

To say they had become friends would be a stretch. But a bond was developing, and each took comfort from the others.

"Mr. Beckett?" Ayisha said.

"Please, call me Alden."

"Okay, Alden. Can I ask you a question?"

"Of course."

"What about people who, because of circumstances beyond their control, have to start off behind?"

"I want to make sure I understand your question," said Alden. "Do you mind going a little deeper into the details?"

Ayisha paused for a moment. "I grew up in an under-resourced inner-city neighborhood. I worked my way through school and was the first person in my family to go to college and earn a degree. I've worked very hard to get ahead, and I've done well in life. I'm a doctor now. I'm proud of the work I do, and I earn a good living."

Ayisha searched for the right words.

"Please . . . go on," Alden said.

"I've always felt frustrated, like the odds were against me. At times," her voice cracked, "it made me very angry."

"How so?"

Ayisha said, "I developed a lot of resentment directed toward more well-to-do people. In college, while my classmates were out having fun, I was always working or studying."

"And today?" asked Alden.

"It's a mixture of emotions. On the one hand, I'm very proud of what I've accomplished. I've earned the success I've had. But there's also a little guilt."

Cordelia asked, "Why the guilt?"

"I'm not sure," said Ayisha. "Maybe guilt's not the right word. I guess I'm feeling . . . responsible?"

"Responsible for what?" Alden asked.

"So many people in my old neighborhood didn't get the same breaks I did—including some in my own family. Maybe I feel a personal duty to help them, especially my mom and a couple of cousins. I feel the need to give back."

Alden nodded. "I can actually relate somewhat."

"How?" Ayisha asked.

"I grew up in a very poor family. Began working full-time jobs at 14. Struggled to pay for school. I too was the first in my family to graduate from college. Like you, I sometimes felt resentful when other kids from wealthier families seemed to have it easier. And I helped my mother financially until she passed."

Bobby watched in silence. *I used that as a pretty good excuse to quit college.*

Alden leaned in. "We have something else in common, too."

"We do? Like what?"

"I too felt a little guilt as my income grew," he said. "I had to work my way through it. Societal messages affected me just like everyone else."

Dylan chuckled. "I wouldn't mind taking on a little of that kind of guilt." The young man waited for a laugh that never came. He looked down and muttered, "Just trying to lighten the mood a little."

"Ayisha," said Alden, "I want to shift your thinking just a little, if I may. You said others you knew didn't get the same breaks you did."

"Right."

Alden smiled. "Ayisha, I don't think you got breaks. I think you made them."

Ayisha said nothing.

Alden looked at the group. "Ayisha's story actually brings us to money truth number five."

5. Money favors the prepared—get in position to win.

"Ayisha took responsibility for her situation, worked very hard, and made a better life."

Alden returned his attention to Ayisha. "You put yourself into a position where you could take advantage of any opportunities that became available to you."

Ayisha shifted in her seat.

Alden said, "Some call that luck. I don't. When you prepare well—getting ready to succeed when the right circumstances come your way—you're not getting lucky . . ."

"But I like getting lucky," said Dylan.

All heads turned.

"What?" He said, "I play the lotto!"

"Moving on," said Alden with a sigh. "Ayisha, you're making your own luck."

Eddie agreed. "There's a picture on my desk that says, 'Success happens when opportunity and preparedness meet.'"

Alden nodded. "It's certainly helpful when breaks come our way. But whether they do, or they don't, the buck stops with us."

"The buck never stops with me," said Dylan. "It goes in one pocket, and out the other." He laughed. "At least I'm keeping that dollar flowing in the river of money!"

Alden smiled. "Dylan, you also have to learn what to do with that buck."

Bobby laughed, barely audible.

"Do some get a head start and have it easier? Yes," said Alden. "But regardless of circumstances, everyone can choose to learn, work hard, and put themselves into a position to succeed. By doing so, they can change their future.

"Ayisha, you're a shining example to the world," Alden said. "Despite some tough circumstances, you hung in there and prevailed. You're a hero—a role model for all of us who grew up in tough situations."

Ayisha smiled.

"But I'd like to encourage you to challenge that belief . . . that you should be giving back. The term *giving back* implies that you owe something and are obligated to pay. Here, you really don't owe anyone. You worked hard, and you prevailed."

Ayisha asked, "Are you saying I shouldn't help?"

"No, no. Not at all," said Alden. "You can still help everyone you want. But you don't need to do so out of a sense of debt or obligation. Instead, you can simply do it because it's what you want to do. It's congruent with your values. And it reflects the type of wonderful and charitable person you are."

Yen agreed. "My niece wants to be a doctor. I'd love for her to meet you someday."

Ayisha nodded.

Alden looked around the vault. "Regardless of the economic situation we grew up in, financial literacy is the ticket to beating the hand we were dealt. That brings us to money truth number six."

6. Money doesn't grow by accident—learn how it works.

"We all need to develop financial literacy," said Alden.

"When you say *financial literacy*," said Cordelia, "what exactly do you mean?"

Alden said, "Basically, it's the ability to learn, understand the importance of, *and use* various financial skills, such as saving, budgeting, investing, and spending. It's personal money management."

"My husband and I haven't been very good at that," said Cacey.

Bobby agreed. *No, we haven't.*

"When people don't use those skills," said Alden, "their risk of bad credit, bankruptcy, and foreclosure goes up. They miss out on the opportunity to create and build wealth. But with a productive money mindset and a few straightforward strategies, you can escape from financial bondage to financial independence."

"You said that earlier, old man," said Dylan. "Gettin' forgetful?"

Alden laughed. "No. Just bears repeating. Plus, it's literally the first thing I tell all my clients. Building wealth becomes much easier when we recognize and change our mistaken beliefs, educate ourselves to become financially literate, and work with a skilled financial advisor."

Bobby looked at Cacey. *I'm sure it's too late for us. Babe, I'm so sorry I've gotten into this mess.*

Eddie added to the lid of the pizza box.

ALDEN'S SEVEN MONEY TRUTHS

1. We are responsible for our money beliefs and actions — choose wisely.

2. Money isn't scarce, even when it feels like it.

3. Money flows like a river — jump in.

4. Childhood and cultural money messages mislead us — challenge them.

5. Money favors the prepared — get in position to win.

6. Money doesn't grow by accident — learn how it works.

Carl walked to the door of the vault and motioned for Bobby to join him and Jamie in the lobby. They gathered around the manager's desk.

"I have an idea," Carl said. "It may be just the thing we need to get out of here."

A more reasoned timbre had replaced the desperation in Carl's voice. Gabrielle was right. His heart was softening . . . a little.

"So, whatcha thinking?" Jamie asked.

Carl turned to Bobby. "We use your wife as a hostage, and get out of here . . ."

"No way!" Bobby said. "She doesn't know it's me. She'd be terrified. And, if it doesn't work, they'll never believe she wasn't in on it. I'm not letting her go to prison. That's not happening!"

"I get it," said Carl. "But it's the only thing I can think of that'll get us out and not force you to leave her behind."

"No!" said Bobby, now in Carl's face. "And let me be really clear about this. Nobody's gonna force me to do anything!"

Carl put his hand on Bobby's shoulder. "Think about it for a bit. It's a good plan. And if we get caught, we'll all agree to tell the cops she had nothing to do with it."

Bobby looked at Carl but said nothing. Finally, he turned and walked away.

After a few steps, he looked back. "If you make me choose, you'll lose."

Bobby entered the vault.

Jamie followed him inside.

Carl muttered, "We'll see about that."

CHAPTER 9

Misguided Stereotypes

2:00 p.m.

The group took a brief break, and people milled around the vault. Dylan and Cordelia were whispering. Eddie and Ayisha were in a conversation as well. Alden could sense their jitters continuing to rise.

Ayisha said, "This feels off to me. I mean, we're in here kinda having a good time and learning things while three armed men are holding us hostage."

Cordelia said, "Should we be doing that? Shouldn't we be worried?"

Alden scanned the room. *Gotta keep 'em talking.*

Alden said, "Actually, it's the best thing we can do right now. Keeping a sense of humor and staying calm keeps things from escalating."

Alden said, "Do you all trust me?"

Eddie immediately piped up. "100 percent." He looked at the others. "We can trust him."

"Then let's keep going. Want to gather back in?"

The hostages complied.

"Earlier," Alden said, "we talked about hidden messages from society and the entertainment industry, and their effect on how we see the world. But much of our perspective also comes from old sayings we've heard throughout our lives, and stereotypes we've repeatedly seen on social media memes and the internet. We often accept them as truth, without even questioning it.

"That brings us to the seventh money truth."

7. Money stereotypes are often wrong—don't blindly believe them.

"What's a saying about money that you've heard repeatedly over your lifetime?" Alden asked.

Cordelia spoke up. "I can answer that one. I can hear my grandma's voice now. 'Money is the root of all evil.' And, my favorite, 'Money can't buy you happiness.'"

Alden laughed. "Maybe money can't buy you happiness. But at least you can be miserable in a better part of town."

Dylan piped up. "I'm not sure if money can buy me happiness or not. But I'm willing to take that chance!"

Everyone laughed.

"My father was a minister," said Eddie. "He always said 'Money is the root of all evil' is a misquoted Bible verse."

Ayisha agreed. "That's right. It's from the book of First Timothy. The actual verse says that it's the *love* of money that's the root of all evil."

Eddie nodded. "Dad said there's nothing wrong with making money. Many heroes of the faith were quite wealthy. But money wasn't their foremost concern. When we love something, or someone, we make choices that give it our highest priority. We forsake all others. When people *love* money, they often mistreat their fellow man . . . or woman.

"Dad said we should *use* money—and *love* people. Greed and crime occur when we do the opposite."

Alden said, "My interpretation of that verse is that it's an unhealthy love of money—an attachment that makes gathering it always your first consideration—that creates the problem."

"Unhealthy?" said Ayisha. "Are you saying there's a *healthy* love of money?"

Alden tilted his head with a raised brow. "When I think of the money I've given to my church, to fund my favorite charities, and used to do things with my family . . . I may not *love* that money," he smiled, "but I certainly like it a lot."

Yen laughed. "I heard a pastor once say, 'If money were the root of all evil . . . don't you think the devil would make us all rich, just so we'd end up in hell with him?'"

Alden chuckled.

"I know one," said Dylan. "The best things in life are free."

Eddie laughed. "Maybe so, but taking care of those best things in life costs money."

Alden agreed. "That's right. And if you're referring to the people you love, money can definitely provide a better future for them."

Alden looked at Cordelia. "Do you think your grandmother was right—that money can't buy you happiness?"

"I think so. But I don't know first-hand." She laughed. "But as soon as I get some, I'll report back to you . . . unless I'm sitting on a beach somewhere, sipping a piña colada."

Alden smiled. "Well, with all due respect to your grandmother, in my opinion, she's only partially correct."

"What do you mean?" Cordelia said.

Alden said, "When we don't have enough money to cover our basic needs, such as food, shelter, clothing, and health care, our stress and anxiety levels rise. That reduces our happiness greatly. But when there's enough cash to cover those necessities, it certainly makes us feel better. From that perspective, money actually *can* buy happiness."

"Grandma's wrong?" Cordelia said, "Good Lord! I'm not telling her. My dad told her she was wrong once, when he was a teenager. He didn't see her for a week!"

"Why not?" asked Dylan.

"His eyes were still swollen." Circling her eyes, she said, "She popped him with a rolling pin. Right there."

Alden laughed. "The same goes for how we perceive our future. When we're saving and investing, and believe we have a certain degree of financial security, it gives us peace of mind."

"Yeah, but I've seen some very unhappy rich people . . . on TV," said Dylan. "My granny and me used to watch her soap operas together. She'd say, 'Bless their hearts. Those rich people sure have a lot of problems, don't they?'"

Alden smirked. "Maybe you should watch a little less TV, Dylan."

Eddie chuckled. "And they can't put anything on television if it isn't true, right?"

Everyone laughed.

"But that brings up a good point," said Alden. "Studies show that when it comes to money above the point of meeting your needs, the difference in happiness is more variable. Greater riches don't always equate to greater contentment."

Jamie pointed at Cordelia. "I like her idea of sitting on a beach somewhere. Now *that* kind of money would make me happy, at least for a while." He winked his comically enlarged eye at Cordelia through his fish-eyed goggles. "Maybe I'll join you."

"Dude!" said Dylan. "Are you seriously hitting on a teller who works at the bank you're robbing?"

Cordelia blushed. Jamie shrugged.

"You're right, Jamie," Alden said. "About that money making you happy—not about flirting with Cordelia. You'd better leave that idea alone."

Alden turned to the group. "When you have extra money to spend doing fun things with friends and family, it can indeed add to happiness. A study of the world's wealthiest people showed those who used resources to create meaningful experiences with loved ones, and support their favorite charitable causes, were indeed happier than those who didn't."

"It's not the money itself," said Eddie, "but how we use it that makes the difference."

Alden agreed. "That's right."

2:15 p.m.

Carl paced around the lobby, trying to think. *What a train wreck this has turned into!*

He snatched up the desk phone.

Inside the Command van, the phone rang.

Kooper grabbed it, and handed the phone to Gabrielle.

"Hi Carl," said Gabrielle. "How's it . . ."

"I want a plane to Mexico."

She paused. "Okay. Carl. Slow down."

Keep him talking.

"Hear me out," said Carl. "I've got a way that you get most of what you want, and we get a little of what we want."

"I'm listening."

"We let all the hostages . . ."

"People, Carl. They're people . . . just like you and me."

She heard Carl take a deep breath. She waited.

After a long beat, Carl said, "Okay, Gabi. *People.* We let all the people go, except one. You get us on a plane to Mexico. We'll release the last *person* at the border."

Gabrielle waited for a moment, then smiled.

"Thank you, Carl."

"Thank me? For what?"

"Instead of making unreasonable demands like some crazy man, you're trying to find a peaceful way out of this. I appreciate that."

"So, you'll do it?"

"I wish I could, Carl. But I can't. That's not the way these things work—except in the movies. The SWAT commander can't let you take anyone with you. But maybe we can figure something else out."

Carl sighed.

"Can I ask you a question?" said Gabrielle.

Keep him talking.

"Sure," said Carl.

"Why are you doing this? You're obviously not a bad guy here. I'm thinking robbing banks isn't your life's calling. So . . . why?"

Gabrielle briefly locked eyes with Kooper and held up crossed fingers.

In hostage situations, they both knew, the brain can quickly descend into fight-or-flight mode, which would almost guarantee sloppy thinking and bad decisions. If she could get Carl looking at reasonable options, it would keep his rational mind in the forefront.

If she couldn't, he might get desperate. And *that* could get ugly.

She held her breath and waited.

Carl sighed again, louder this time.

"So, I got into a lot of financial trouble a few years back and declared bankruptcy."

Gabrielle let out her breath and gave Kooper a thumbs-up.

"My wife and me divorced over it. It was brutal. Texas is supposed to be a community property state, but she got almost everything. I even lost visitation rights with my kids. The judge said I was a . . ." His voice broke, and he cleared his throat. "A bad influence."

"I'm so sorry, Carl."

Carl said, "So, now I'm broke. I'm broken-hearted. And I have very little to lose here, Gabi."

"Carl," said Gabrielle. "Situation like that? I can see how that would make anyone feel desperate. Those are some tough things to go through. But may I disagree with you on one little thing?"

Carl dropped into his chair like a teenager, prepping for a parent's lecture. "Fine."

"You actually do have something to lose."

"Yeah? What?"

"How many children do you have, Carl?"

"Three. They're six, 10, and 13."

"Carl, *that's* what you have to lose. You may not have them today, but that can change. You can send them notes. Call them. Someday, when they're adults, you'll get the chance to mend those relationships."

Carl said nothing.

Gabrielle said, "And there are ways to stay out of those financial problems in the future, too. I was in a deep hole myself, years ago. A friend showed me how to dig out of that hole, and stay out. If I learned how to do that, you can too."

She heard Carl sigh again.

"Don't lose hope on me, Carl. I care about what happens to you. We'll get you through this. And we'll do it in a way that gives you the chance at a future with your kids.

"All we have to do is get everyone out of there safely . . . including you."

As Bobby and Jamie listened, Alden posed a question to the group. "What about stereotypes?"

Jamie said, "We used to have some *stereo type* when I was a kid." He laughed. "It played vinyl."

The room fell silent.

"What? Nothing?" said Jamie.

Bobby shook his head. *Nice job, Joke Whisperer. Great delivery.*

The hostages looked around, unsure of how to react. Finally, Eddie made hand gestures as if playing an air drum set. "Ba-dump–ching."

Ayisha smirked and shrugged. "Man, some bank robbers just can't tell a joke. Turns out armed and hilarious is harder than it looks. Might want to drop the whole mic and gun thing."

Jamie laughed. "So, you're saying my set ended half an hour ago, and I should get off the stage?"

Ayisha nodded. "Right after we throw tomatoes. Mind if we pay our checks and hit the exits?"

Alden smirked. "Seriously, what are the stereotypes that affect how you see money?"

Dylan started. "Rich people are dishonest."

"Poor people are lazy," said Ayisha.

Cacey raised her hand to chest level and wiggled her fingers. "Women are bad with money."

Bobby dropped his head. *Sorry for saying that, babe.*

"When I hear stereotypes about anything," said Alden, "whether it's people, things, or money, I find it best to hold two sentences in mind. They keep me from mentally tossing everyone into the same bucket." Alden trailed off, lost in thought.

"Well, don't leave us hanging there, Alden." Eddie said, "What are they?"

Alden held up one finger and said, "Some are." Holding up the second finger, he added, "Most aren't."

Alden said, "Are rich people dishonest? Some are. Most aren't. Are poor people lazy? Some are. Most aren't. Are women bad with money? Are men bad with money? Some are. Most aren't."

Alden smiled. "Are all men in a wheelchair extra sexy?" Lifting his hands, he said, "Some are . . ."

The group laughed.

Ayisha said, "Now *that's* how to tell a joke."

Alden said, "Just remember, anytime we make general assumptions about any group . . . we're going to be wrong. It doesn't matter if it relates to money, race, gender, or anything else. The truth is usually, some are, but most aren't."

Eddie scribbled on the pizza box. "If this goes on much longer, we're going to need more pizza boxes."

ALDEN'S SEVEN MONEY TRUTHS

1. We are responsible for our money beliefs and actions — choose wisely.

2. Money isn't scarce, even when it feels like it.

3. Money flows like a river – jump in.

4. Childhood and cultural money messages mislead us — challenge them.

5. Money favors the prepared — get in position to win.

6. Money doesn't grow by accident — learn how it works.

7. Money stereotypes are often wrong – don't blindly believe them.

Abbondanza Pizza

Kooper slid a chair over to Gabrielle, who was still on the phone with Carl. He mouthed, *You getting tired?*

She nodded, stretched her neck, and sat down.

Over 90 percent of hostage negotiations end safely. Strategically, a negotiator using patience and conversation proves much more effective than pressure and confrontation.

Could that make things take a while? Of course. As a matter of fact, Gabrielle's longest hostage situation lasted for 18 hours—before coming to a successful conclusion.

Kooper and Gabrielle stared at the screen. Carl's demeanor change was giving them hope that this course of action was working, and a peaceful resolution wouldn't be far away.

She just needed to keep the conversation going.

"Carl, can I tell you something?"

"Okay."

"I used to be on the SWAT team in Dallas. Worked there for 10 years."

"I have family in the Dallas/Fort Worth area," said Carl.

"Oh, *please* tell me I didn't meet any of them in a similar situation."

Carl laughed. "No. Two uncles. One's a preacher. The other's a lawyer."

Gabrielle smirked. "A preacher and a lawyer? What happened to you?"

Carl softly laughed. "I know, right?"

"Criminal lawyer?" Gabrielle asked.

"Yeah. Why?"

"Carl, that's great. He can help us mitigate all this for you."

Carl sighed. "Maybe."

He asked, "Why'd you leave the big city to come to this small town?"

"Oh, lots of reasons, I guess. The job kept getting more and more dangerous. The cost of living was higher. I finally decided I'd had enough."

Gabrielle carefully weighed what she was planning to say next.

"That's not the entire story, Carl."

"Tell me."

Kooper raised his brows. What sounded like genuine interest in Carl's voice surprised him.

Gabrielle pointed to the screen. The video quality was excellent, and she could clearly see Carl's expression. He had removed his sunglasses and pushed the black scarf up off of his forehead.

It matched his voice.

"I had another situation like this one," said Gabrielle. "Not in a bank. Just a despondent father in a mobile home. He was going under, financially, and had lost his children."

"Sounds familiar."

"Not exactly. He lost his children in an accident. There was no way for him to get those relationships back."

"Oh . . . wow."

"I'd never lost anyone up to that day, Carl. I always found a way to help people out of whatever situation they were in."

"What happened?"

Gabi sighed. "He told me goodbye, continued to hold the phone to his ear as he walked out the door, and pointed an empty gun at the officers."

She waited.

Carl was silent.

"Carl, they fired."

Kooper watched the screen as Carl dropped his head.

"Carl, I don't think you want anybody to get hurt. I suspect your guns may be empty, too. Please don't make me go through that again. I'll help you find a way out. You, and Jamie, and Bobby can all walk out of there safely. We can do this. I'll even put in a good word with the district attorney—tell her how helpful you were."

"You'd do that?"

"Yes. I would."

Carl didn't reply. He simply hung up the phone and stared through the lobby doors.

He leaned forward onto the desk, closed his eyes, and rested his face in his palms. His head pounded. The warmth of his hands reminded him of hot barber towels wrapped snugly around his brow and cheeks—a luxury he hadn't splurged for in quite some time.

His head popped up.

Wait a minute!

He sat there, confused, eyes moving across the room.

How'd she know the guns weren't loaded? Or the names Bobby and Jamie?

His stare froze—straight ahead.

He shot up out of the chair, knocking it over, and stormed toward the vault.

Dylan stood to stretch his legs. Eddie grabbed the last slice of pizza. And Cordelia noticed Jamie's goggle-enlarged eyes looking her way—blinking.

Alden noticed, too.

Alden said, "Jamie, why don't you give Cordelia a . . ."

Before he could finish, Carl exploded into the vault. He took off his sunglasses and head covering and threw them on the floor.

Alden turned. *Uh-oh.*

Carl glared at Alden and said, "It's you, isn't it?"

Unlock THE VAULT

Secure the **combination** to access your **FREE Resources**

Visit **www.HiddenHeistVault.com** to claim your exclusive access to The Vault - a treasure trove of complimentary guides and insights.

If you experience any difficulty registering for The Vault, please email **support@referralcoach.com**

CHAPTER 10

It's You, Isn't It?

2:25 p.m.

"It's you, isn't it?"

Alden asked, "What's me?"

"SWAT's been a step ahead of us this whole time. They knew there was plenty of water in the cooler. Used our names. She seems to have all the answers. And I think it's you feeding them to her!"

Okay. Gotta calm him down.

"Cameras in the bank?" Alden smiled. "Hey, maybe Jamie told them your names!"

The phone in Alden's wheelchair buzzed. He didn't move. He ignored the vibration.

Unfortunately, Carl heard. He held out his hand, palm up, not saying a word.

Alden reached under his leg and grabbed the hidden phone. He sighed and surrendered it.

> Update . . .
> Carl seems to want a peaceful way out.

> **Not a bad guy. Just desperate. You agree? Any news in there?**

The intensity in Carl's voice returned.

"Who *are* you?"

Alden said nothing.

Carl moved his face within inches of Alden's. With a voice lowered in decibels, but raised in edge, he said again, "Who . . . are . . . you?"

Alden conceded.

"Name's Alden Beckett. I used to be the SWAT team commander and hostage negotiator here."

Murmurs filled the vault.

"A little over 10 years ago, a bullet in my spine caused an unplanned career change."

Dylan whispered to Eddie, "He's a cop?"

"*Was* a cop. Shh . . ." said Eddie.

"You know Gabi?" Carl asked.

Alden nodded. "Worked together in Dallas. She replaced me here. I still work with her now—I'm her financial advisor."

Alden watched Carl's face redden.

Keep him talking.

"Look, Carl, stay calm. This is a good thing."

"How's this a good thing?"

"I'm well versed in SWAT protocols. If you'll work with me, I can help. We can get you, and everyone else, out of this in one piece."

Carl looked back through all the messages.

He replied to Gabrielle.

Gabrielle looked at her incoming message, exhaled a slow, long breath, and dropped her head.

"What?" asked Kooper.

She handed him the phone.

> News?
> Yes.
> I now have the phone instead of Beckett.
> Carl

Kooper read the text. "Uh-oh. What now?"

She gave a one-word reply. "Alden."

Law enforcement technology has propelled progress over the years. Robotics, drones, and the ability to tap into live footage have given police a house advantage that is much greater than any casino. But Alden taught Gabrielle, with hostage negotiation—it's still an old-world skill. It requires empathy, tact, and the ability to see the criminal's perspective first, then gently reframe their point of view to arrive at a positive outcome.

Alden Beckett had been one of the very best. He still was.

Alden gave Gabrielle hope.

Those same skills were also why he was now successful as a financial advisor. They helped him shift how people viewed money. Then he could guide them into a much better financial future.

"Carl, let me ask you a question," said Alden. "If you don't think they're just going to let you go, how would you like to see this end? What do you see as a win for you guys?"

"I don't know."

"Mind if I make a suggestion?" asked Alden.

Carl said nothing.

"What do you think about maybe letting the others out first? I'll stay in here with you. Then, whenever you think the time's right, the three of you can roll me out, staying safely behind me. If you lay your guns down, they'll never shoot you. Especially with me in front. We can let Gabi know what we're doing. She'll control things outside. She's really good at her job."

"Because you trained her?" Carl scoffed.

Alden said nothing.

Carl said, "I'll think it over. But remember this." He touched Yen's revolver, now in his waistband, and said, "She may know our guns aren't loaded, but this one is."

He left the vault.

Jamie followed him.

Gabrielle said, "Ring 'em."

With a few keystrokes, Kooper called the lobby phone.

Carl answered. "Yeah?"

"How ya doin', Carl?"

"I've had luckier days. How the heck did we pick a bank where a SWAT team commander was in the lobby?"

"I don't know, Carl. But that actually *is* pretty lucky, though."

"How?"

"Look, Alden taught me everything I know. He always saw the potential good in people, and he was forever focused on finding a peaceful solution—often in very creative ways. He can help us figure out a safe way through this."

"Maybe," Carl said. "But I was starting to trust you. That's gone."

He slammed the phone into the cradle.

Gabrielle sighed and looked at Kooper.

"I hope I didn't just lose him."

"As a financial advisor, my job is leadership. I define that as helping people make educated financial decisions that are in their best interest—that they wouldn't make without the right advice."

—Alden Beckett

CHAPTER 11

The Value of a Financial Professional

2:30 p.m.

Ayisha said, "You're a cop?"

"*Was* a cop," said Alden. "Had to find a new career after ending up in this chair. I'd worked with a good financial advisor over my years in the department. She helped me build a nice nest egg. So, when I was looking for a new direction, I became an advisor, myself. We're all happier when we believe our work is meaningful. Helping people build a better financial future fulfills that desire in me."

Dylan looked at Eddie. "You knew *Mr. Beckett* was a cop?"

Eddie nodded.

"Me too," said Yen.

Dylan turned to Alden. "You're a cop with a nest egg? You *must've* been on the take. Any cop with a lot of money has to be crooked!"

Alden slowly shook his head. "Dylan . . . some are. Most aren't."

"So, how'd you get your money if you're an honest cop?" Dylan asked.

"Was . . . an honest cop," said Alden.

"It wasn't all that complicated. Once I realized I didn't know how to manage my money, I got help. My advisor guided me to correct my mistaken beliefs and unhelpful habits about money. And she encouraged me to become a student . . . to develop my own financial literacy. She said, 'Financial confidence comes with financial competence.'"

Cordelia asked, "So, what'd she have you do?"

"We focused on a few simple and straightforward strategies—things I could do even on a cop's salary. Small steps, which I repeated every month. I made a list, posted them on my refrigerator and desk, and referred to them as The Laws for Financial Independence."

"Laws?" said Cacey. "With your background? Seems fitting."

Alden laughed. "Maybe that's where the idea came from. I'm certainly one for following the laws. I also developed some additional income streams. Nothing huge. Just more ways to get into the flow of money."

Ayisha smirked. "Being a financial advisor in down times can make you pretty unpopular. Think you'll get shot again?"

Alden grimaced. "Let's hope not. Realistically, most people know, as valuable as a financial professional can be, they have absolutely no control of the stock market or the economy. Nobody's *that* good."

"Excuse me, Mr. Alden," said Cacey in a soft voice. "I think what you meant to say is *some* are. *Most* aren't."

Alden couldn't help himself. Her sweet smile and demure demeanor disarmed him completely. He laughed. "Point taken."

Bobby smiled beneath his mask.

"The stock market is like a person walking up a flight of stairs with a yo-yo," said Alden. "Up and down in the short run—but always up in the long run."

Eddie laughed. "Alden, I think of you like a cowboy's bronc-reins at the rodeo. You can't control which way a horse is heading. But you help me stay in the saddle when the market bucks and twists."

"Sounds scary to me," Dylan said.

"I understand," said Alden. "But it would be scarier to miss out on the growth you'd see from investing for the long term. That's why finding a professional is key to building a solid financial future. They'll help you pick a strategy that's right for you and mitigates your risks."

Ayisha said, "Does working with a financial advisor really make that much of a difference?"

"It does," Alden said. "As a matter of fact, a well-respected financial survey showed 75 percent of people who work with a financial advisor feel secure about their retirement. Only 45 percent for those who don't feel the same. And those who'd worked with an advisor had saved twice as much money."

Jamie returned to the vault. "I was really starting to enjoy this. What'd I miss?"

"Alden told a joke," said Dylan. "It started with, 'Three bank robbers and a retired SWAT guy rolled into a bank . . .' Wait! Have you heard this one already?"

Jamie laughed and gestured around the room. "Dude! That sounds just like this! How'd it end?"

Bobby hit Jamie on the shoulder. *Idiot!*

Alden dropped his eyes. *Bless his heart. You can fix ignorance with knowledge. But dumbass may be permanent.*

Jamie laughed. "Holy smokes! This scene reminds me of high school. Are you guys all in class, or what?"

"Detention," said Ayisha.

"I loved detention!" Dylan said. "Best times of my high school career—six awesome years—happened in detention! That's where I met my first wife—and my second!"

"You've been married twice?" asked Eddie.

"No. Just once. But I've got the next one picked out. She just doesn't know it yet. Plus, I have to wait. She ain't exactly single. And I don't want her husband ticked off at me. He's a big ol' boy!"

Cordelia shook her head. "Why are we not surprised about that?"

Jamie looked at Alden. "So, Beckett, is that how you ended up in that chair? Somebody's husband get ticked at you?"

Alden grinned. "Not exactly."

"Well, what happened?"

Alden said, "A domestic disturbance case. The man had barricaded himself into a house. He'd stolen a neighbor's handgun . . ." Alden's voice trailed off.

"Please keep going," said Cacey. "I'd like to hear this."

Alden nodded. "He wasn't a hardened criminal. He had no experience with guns." Raising a brow at Bobby and Jamie, he said, "Kinda like you guys."

Alden said, "He was about to surrender to me. I told him to put the gun down, but he was nervous and held onto it. As he stepped off the porch, the guy stumbled—bumped the ground hard. When he did, his finger was still on the trigger, and he accidentally discharged the weapon. Unfortunately, the bullet nailed me. Nicked my spine."

In unison, the group winced.

Alden looked around the room. "By the way, if any of you in here own a gun, *never* allow your finger to touch the trigger unless you intend to destroy what's in front of the sight. And always consider a gun as being loaded—even when it's not. Keep it pointed in a safe direction."

"So, you're teaching us a gun safety course now too?" said Dylan.

"He actually does teach a gun safety class," Eddie said.

Dylan said, "Really?"

Alden shrugged. "Who better?"

"Man," said Jamie. "Getting shot that way sucks!"

"Yeah, no kidding. Sucked for the other guy, too. He took two bullets in the arm, and his domestic disturbance charge jumped to a first-degree felony."

Alden paused for a moment. "Jamie, you and Bobby need to make sure that nothing like that happens here today. It'll make things much worse."

Jamie took off his head covering. "I guess we don't need these anymore." Rings, created by the goggles, prominently circled his eyes.

He looked at Bobby. "You taking yours off?"

Bobby said nothing. He slowly shook his head.

"What made you decide to become a hostage negotiator?" said Ayisha.

Eddie smiled. "I'd like to hear that too. As long as we've known each other, I've never heard the story."

Alden recounted his story. "I didn't plan to go that way. Got my start as a police officer in a prison. Had a pretty terrible reputation."

"What do you mean?" Jamie asked.

"Well, let's just say I wasn't always seeking a peaceful solution. I looked for trouble—and usually found it. I'd ask for all the hard cases. Then I'd say things . . . do things, just to get the guy to throw a punch. Someone once said, if Mother Teresa came into my unit, I could get her to take a swing at me within the first five minutes."

Alden shook his head. He sighed with a perspective hindsight often brings. "I took that as a compliment."

"Man," said Dylan. "Even I wouldn't have done that. I'd get my butt kicked too often."

"So, what made you change?" Ayisha asked.

"I heard, through the back channels, the other officers didn't want to work with me anymore because I was always getting into fights. They thought it was too dangerous—and they were right. So, I chose a different path. I intentionally worked on my people skills, took a few classes, and developed the ability to talk with people in such a way that, instead of creating problems—we found solutions."

He shrugged. "At that point, I still asked for all the hard cases, but to see if I could talk them down and get the situation resolved peacefully. Turned out I was good at it. All of that eventually led me to become a hostage negotiator."

"You've always seemed so calm to me," said Yen. "I can't imagine you being a troublemaker. But the talking people out of trouble part . . . I can definitely see that."

"Right," said Alden. "I still do, I guess. But now, I'm attempting to talk people out of the financial trouble they'll find if they don't shift their beliefs and habits when it comes to their relationship with money. When we can change their thoughts—they can change their decisions and actions. And their new behaviors will give them a chance at a more secure future."

Carl picked up the phone, ringing the Command van.

Kooper put his headset on and pointed to Gabrielle.

Gabrielle answered. "Hi Carl."

Carl said, "Gabi, I'm tired of all this. I want a car that holds four people, an escort to the Brenham airport, and a pilot ready when we get there."

"The Brenham airport?" said Gabrielle. "Carl, a plane from there can't get you to Mexico. Not enough fuel."

She paused to let the comment sink in. "You sound more tired and stressed than before. Has something changed?"

Carl said, "It's 2:47. You have one hour and 13 minutes."

He broke off the call.

"The first bill you pay every month should be to your savings or investment account. Saving up front will shine a light on spending habits that no longer serve you."

—Alden Beckett

CHAPTER 12

Financial Independence, One Law at a Time

3:00 p.m.

Bobby peered into the lobby. Carl was no longer pacing back and forth. He wasn't kicking things.

Instead, he was sitting on the sofa next to the branch manager's desk, his head leaning back.

Good. Maybe he's calming down.

Bobby took a couple of steps closer to get a better look. His welcome discovery quickly faded into unwanted distress.

Scratch that!

Carl began rocking. Staring ahead at nothing—his lips moving as if in angry conversation.

Bobby positioned himself at the vault opening and motioned for Jamie to join him.

Ayisha said, "Alden, I make a nice income, but I'm not rich by any definition. What do you think I should do now?"

"That's a perfect question, Ayisha," said Alden.

She smiled. "Thank you."

"My pleasure."

"First, don't focus too much on becoming 'rich' or 'wealthy,'" Alden said. "Those terms get us emotionally focused on a dollar figure. We think, 'I'll be rich when I have a million dollars in the bank.' Or, 'I'll be wealthy when I own this or that.'"

Jamie nudged Bobby. "That sounds pretty good to me!"

Bobby ignored the comment and kept his eyes locked on Carl.

Cordelia asked, "So, what should we focus on?"

"Focus on financial independence," said Alden.

"Explain, please," said Yen.

"Financial independence is all about freedom," Alden said. "Living life on your own terms. It gives you the opportunity to expand your choices. If you have enough money to support the life you want, and enough free time to enjoy using the money you have, in my opinion, you really are wealthy. And with that comes the independence and freedom."

In the lobby, Carl muttered something unintelligible, as he began pacing again.

Bobby's pulse quickened.

"For some," said Alden, "that may mean having enough income coming in, without working, to fund their passion for travel and seeing their family. For others like me, who love what they do, it may be the freedom to do the work we want . . . only we're the boss. I hand pick my clients and set my own schedule."

"Can that really be done—by just anybody?" asked Dylan.

"Yes, it can. It's not overly complicated."

"You make it sound so easy," said Cacey.

Alden smiled. "Easy? Not always. But simple for sure. Start with small steps in the right direction. Then repeat them daily."

"So," said Ayisha, "how do we get moving on this?"

Alden circled his finger. "Although none of us would have chosen to be in this vault today, this is actually a pretty good way to begin. Become aware of how your mistaken beliefs are limiting your financial future and embrace the truths about money. Then take action—learn and implement some straightforward financial principles. And finally, get some help."

Cordelia said, "So, what are those Laws for Financial Independence?"

"Wait a minute," said Eddie. "I need the second pizza box to take notes."

Cordelia passed Eddie the box as Alden began to teach.

"I consider the first three laws as laying the foundation. The first law is . . ."

1. Pick a financial pro to mentor you.

"Some refer to themselves as financial planners or wealth managers. In my case—I'm a financial advisor," said Alden. "Find one who fits you best, and work with them."

Dylan chuckled. "So sayeth the financial advisor."

Alden smiled. "It doesn't have to be me. But you need someone who knows how to help you hit your goals. Eventually, you may add an accountant, an estate planning attorney, and possibly an insurance specialist. They'll help you earn a solid return, limit your tax liability, and protect your legacy. The goal? Living life on your own terms."

"I was hesitant at first,' said Eddie. "Heck, I'm a bank manager. I thought getting financial advice would make me look incompetent. But I learned that getting help isn't a sign of weakness. It shows strength."

Alden said, "My job is financial leadership. I define that as helping people make educated financial decisions that are in their best interest—that they wouldn't make without the right advice. It's the most important thing I do, and why my career feels like a calling to me instead of just a job. Find a financial professional you trust, listen to them, then follow the plan the two of you develop."

"So, how do we find one?" asked Cordelia.

"If you don't know one personally, start asking around." Alden laughed. "But ask people who are financially where you want to be in life."

Jamie chuckled, "So, you're saying if you have the choice of asking rich people or broke people for financial advice—ask the rich people." He looked around the vault. "That means none of you'll be asking me."

Alden laughed. "I probably wouldn't have said it that way . . . but yeah, I guess that's right. That would be like asking me about car repairs—a subject about which I'm clueless."

Dylan raised his hand. "I'm your guy on that one."

"Look," said Alden, "we all have well-meaning people in our lives who are more than willing to share advice on making money. Unfortunately, many have lots of advice, but very little money. And even if they've done well, rather than asking for financial advice, ask for the name of their financial advisor. You don't need tips. You need a guide who knows what they're doing, and you can build a relationship with."

Cordelia laughed. "My cousin is the smartest financial guy I know. He lives in a run-down mobile home with the floor falling out. But he knows how to invest! Just ask him!"

Eddie chuckled. "I've got a friend who has $75,000 in credit card debt and can't keep a job. He needs a financial advisor!"

Alden smiled and said, "Actually, he needs debt counseling . . . and therapy."

Everyone laughed.

"There are lots of financial advisors and resources available for getting the right guidance," said Alden.

"I don't make enough money to work with a financial advisor," said Cordelia. "I don't have a nest egg."

Alden nodded. "I understand what you mean. I used to think that too because some advisors only work with people who meet a pretty high minimum portfolio threshold."

Dylan nudged Eddie. "A high what?"

"Wealthy people."

"Oh. Yeah, right."

"Others," said Alden, "like my first financial advisor and me, have a passion for helping us more ordinary people build our wealth."

Cordelia nodded.

"Getting expert advice," Alden said, "can definitely be the difference-maker. You don't have to make a huge amount of money to accumulate lasting wealth for you and your family—and even future generations. I'm a perfect example."

"I'll start, eventually," said Dylan. "But I'm too young to worry about that right now. Plus, I don't want some dude," nodding to Ayisha, he added, "or *dude-ette*, telling me what I can or can't do with my money."

Alden smiled. "Is that what you think a financial advisor does?"

"Yep. That's exactly what I think."

Alden paused. "You're a bright young man. But that youth comes with a lack of experience. Are you open to the thoughts of a man who *used* to be young?"

Dylan folded his arms and leaned back. "Sure, old man. Go ahead."

"First off," Alden said, "it's never too soon, or too late, to make the right financial decisions. And since you're so young, you can take advantage of some simple principles for a much longer period. The results you'll get will be outstanding."

Dylan said nothing.

"And second, a financial advisor doesn't tell you what you can or can't do with your money. Instead, they help you develop a plan to achieve the goals you want for your future. Then they make sure you understand the trade-offs with any financial decisions you make. They basically help you live life as your own adventure . . . just with your eyes open."

The lobby phone rang.

"Hi Carl. Just wanted to update you. There weren't any planes at the Brenham airport that could make the trip. We're checking around the other airports in the area."

Gabrielle was lying to Carl for the first time. She had no intention of getting them a plane.

Carl said, "Forty-nine minutes," and hung up the phone.

Kooper asked Gabrielle, "Want me to get the sniper into position?"

She sighed. "Position? Yes. But nobody makes a move unless it's under my direct order. I'm not giving up on him yet."

"So, what's the second law?" Dylan asked.

Alden asked a question of the group. "When you get your paycheck, how do you decide who to pay first?"

Jamie chuckled. "The bill collector who yells the loudest?"

"Not me," said Dylan, laughing. "I had a bill collector get rude to me once. I told him, 'Listen, dude! I decide which bills to pay by putting all of 'em in a hat—then drawing them out, one by one. I pay them in the order I pull them. When the money runs out, I'm through.'

"The guy asked me, 'So what?' I said, 'So what? That means if you're a jerk—you don't even go into the hat next month!'"

Everyone laughed.

Alden said, "Let me shift your thinking about that. The first person you should pay each month may surprise you."

Alden looked at Eddie. "Tell 'em, Eddie."

Eddie said, "It's you. Law number two is . . ."

2. Pay yourself first.

"That's right," said Alden. "Pick a dollar amount, or a percentage of what you earn, and put that money into savings and investments. Have it deducted from your paycheck before you ever get the money. Your savings will be for more immediate needs. And investments will be for your future."

"How much do you think we should put back?" asked Cordelia.

"Make it stretch you a little," said Alden. "Whatever amount you think you can do . . . do a little more. I start my clients off thinking in the 10 to 20 percent range."

"My dad knew all about savings," Eddie said. "He was good at it. But he never really got the investing part."

"I understand," said Alden. "The trouble is, when you don't invest, it drastically limits your potential for a secure financial future."

Ayisha said, "Alden, no disrespect, but I disagree with that one. My first 10 percent goes to my church. I tithe."

Alden smiled. "I understand. I do the same thing. So, we pay ourselves after. But since we consider that first 10 percent His anyway, we really are paying ourselves first—just from the portion we consider ours."

Ayisha nodded.

"I also have clients who have no particular faith or religion but still give their first 10 percent to charities they love," Alden said.

Ayisha nodded. "The more we give, the more we seem to get blessed."

Alden agreed.

Then he kept moving. "Law number three is . . ."

3. Establish an emergency fund.

"Use your savings to build up money for when life hands you surprises along the way. Put the money into an account you can't spend from easily."

Eddie agreed. "Like a savings account—not checking. You want to be able to access it in an emergency, but not so easily that you could spend it on impulse."

"How much do you recommend we keep in an emergency fund?" said Ayisha.

"That depends on your situation," said Alden. "The last statistic I heard is around 37 percent of Americans can't even cover an unexpected car repair of $400."

"That wouldn't be a problem," said Ayisha.

Dylan piped up. "Is for me. As a matter of fact, it happened earlier this year. Had to put it on the credit card."

Bobby looked at Cacey. *Would be a problem for us too.*

Alden continued. "For most people on a salary, I recommend having readily available cash that's at least three months' worth of income. But if you work for yourself . . ."

"And I do," said Ayisha.

"Then I recommend an amount equal to at least six months of your income and expenses. This will take some time, but it's well worth it. That's also an area where your advisor may steer you toward certain insurance products such as disability and business insurance."

Ayisha nodded. "That makes sense. As a matter of fact, I just increased my disability insurance because my income rose last year."

"Excellent. Not everyone thinks to do that," said Alden. "Disability insurance helps but often leaves a gap. Your emergency fund will help make up the difference."

"Besides disability, what other types of insurance products would you recommend?" Eddie asked.

Alden thought. "That varies from client to client. But, at a minimum, I recommend health insurance, or at least a health-share organization, a long-term care policy to cover nursing home care, life insurance . . ."

"Life insurance?" said Dylan. "Not me! I don't want people getting rich off me dying!"

Alden smiled with the patience of a father trying to teach his wayward son.

"Dylan, you buy life insurance so you can make sure those you love aren't facing tremendous financial burdens because you're not here anymore. You're single now. So, maybe you get enough to make sure that your parents wouldn't have to pay your final expenses. Eventually, you'll get married . . ."

"Again," Dylan said with a smile.

Alden nodded. "Yes, again. And you may have children . . ."

"That's scary," said Ayisha.

Alden chuckled. "Though we all hate to think about dying, life insurance can make sure your wife and children have enough money to cover their living expenses in your absence."

Cordelia asked, "How much should we get?"

"As a general rule," said Alden, "five to ten times your annual income is the standard advice. Talk with your financial advisor or insurance specialist to discuss your specific situation."

Gabrielle's radio squawked.

"SWAT Command, this is Helo November Four Zero Niner Tango, X-Ray, approximately one-quarter mile south of your position. Requesting permission to . . ."

Gabrielle grabbed the radio and yelled, "No!"

"The most valuable asset you'll ever own is your ability to grow and improve. Building your knowledge and skills is an investment that pays lifelong dividends. Investing in yourself is risk-free growth."

—Alden Beckett

CHAPTER 13

Breaking Free

3:15 p.m.

Carl was sitting at the bank manager's desk when he heard the noise. A rapid *whoosh, whoosh, whoosh, whoosh.*

He rushed to the lobby doors and peeked outside.

Gabrielle saw the panicked look on his face.

Bobby heard the commotion and went into the lobby. Alden and Jamie followed.

"What is that?" asked Jamie.

The mechanical slicing through the air continued.

Pulsing.

Rhythmic.

The helicopter was getting louder and closer by the second.

Carl yelled, "Get down!"

Jamie ducked behind a desk. "Are they trying to get in position for a clean shot at us?"

Carl paced, looking first at Alden, then back out the window to see the helicopter.

"I don't like this! We haven't hurt anybody." He pointed at Alden. "You said they wouldn't come in as long as nobody gets hurt."

"I still think that's right."

"Well, what's happening here?" Carl's face turned a deep red.

Before Alden could answer, the lobby phone rang.

Alden picked up the handset.

"Gabi, this is Alden. What's going on?"

He listened, looking occasionally at Carl, nodding, trying to reassure him.

"Okay. I'll tell them."

Alden said, "By the way, Gabi, I suggested a possible solution to Carl. I asked about the idea of letting everyone else go on out, but I'd stay. Then, after the others are safe, the three of them could come out behind me. Told him I was reasonably sure that nobody out there dislikes me enough to shoot through me to get to them."

He listened.

Alden smirked. "Ha-ha. Very funny. I'll tell him."

He hung up.

Carl raised his eyebrows as he saw Alden's face.

Alden pointed upward. "News station helicopter out of Houston. Gabi's getting them to move off."

"What else?" said Carl.

Alden smirked. "Oh, yeah. She said she'd guarantee your safety, but as for me—no promises."

Bobby and Jamie laughed with a sigh of relief.

"I can see how she might think that," said Carl. "Thought about shooting you more than once today myself."

Alden smiled. "Well, I'm glad you didn't. You'd have ruined my new shirt."

Alden gave Carl a comforting look. "Carl, I know you're getting nervous. But as long as this doesn't go on much longer, and you don't hurt anybody, they won't storm the place. We can get everybody out safely if you'll work with me. But it would be a good idea to consider doing that sooner rather than later—before SWAT Command takes over."

Carl said nothing.

Alden, Bobby, and Jamie returned to the vault.

Ayisha met Alden, Bobby, and Jamie at the vault door. Dylan and Eddie followed.

Ayisha said, "What's happening out there? When are we getting out of here?"

"Soon," Alden said. "I think it won't be much longer. We just need to stay . . ."

"Calm?" said Dylan. "That ship's sailed. I'm about ready to just make a break for it."

Bobby touched Dylan on the arm and whispered, "Please don't."

Alden looked at Bobby, then back to Dylan, Ayisha, and Eddie.

"Bobby's right," Alden said. "Let's keep our cool for just a little longer."

He nodded toward the chairs, and the three hostages took their seats.

Okay. Gotta keep 'em thinking about other things.

Alden began again. "Okay, the last three laws are about accelerating your results. Law number four is . . ."

4. Budget your spending.

"Veteran financial journalist Charles A. Jaffe says, 'Live within your needs . . . not within your means. It's not your salary that makes you rich; it's your spending habits.' He's absolutely correct."

"I've tried that before," said Cordelia. "I even put money in envelopes for each category of expenses. I failed miserably."

"Well, don't get too down on yourself," Alden said. "Many struggle with this. But failing once doesn't mean you shouldn't try again. You may succeed this time."

Eddie laughed. "Reminds me of my college entrance exams." He held up three fingers, and said, "Had to take the SAT three times to score high enough to get into Baylor."

Alden smiled. "Speak with an advisor on this. Some are big believers in budgeting and tracking every penny. That's a valid way to go. If that's just not something you can do, at least make sure that you're aware of your spending and you prioritize where the money goes."

Alden nodded to Dylan. "You remember that Warren Buffett guy?"

Dylan smirked. "You kidding? We grabbed a beer together at the Broken Bone Saloon just last Saturday."

Alden laughed. "Well, tell him hello from me, next time you see him."

Dylan said, "Will do."

"He advises everyone, regardless of their income and financial situation—don't save what's left after spending. Instead, spend what's left after saving."

Dylan nodded. "Yep. That's Warren, alright."

Alden smiled. *His goofy comments are actually helping.*

Alden finished the point. "Spend a little less than you think you should. And save and invest a little more than you think you can."

Alden moved on. "Law number five is . . ."

5. Get rid of credit card and high-interest debt.

Cordelia and Yen winced.

Ayisha said, "Not an easy thing to do, especially if you ever get behind. How do you suggest we do that?"

"First, build that emergency fund," said Alden. "Then each month, after you pay your monthly needs—allocate every additional dollar to paying off your consumer and credit card debts. Start with the obligation that has the smallest balance. Put every extra dollar you earn toward paying off that single account. Once it's paid off, add that monthly payment, plus any extra you can swing, to paying off the next debt with the lowest balance. Then just keep repeating the process."

Bobby looked at Cacey. *We could've done that while I was working.*

"Once you pay off a few debts, you'll be amazed at how much extra money you can dedicate to paying off the rest each month. Eventually, your debts will be gone.

"Just remember, you can't get ahead if you're using a large portion of your income paying interest."

"That happened to us," Cacey said.

Alden nodded. "Happens to a lot of people."

"What do you recommend for larger purchases?" asked Eddie.

"I recommend opening a separate account and saving for such items, like appliances and vehicles. Consider waiting until you've accumulated enough money to pay cash before you buy."

"Wow," said Cordelia. "That means I'd never have a car or a TV."

"You can if you're okay with making some different choices," said Alden.

"What do you mean?"

Alden said, "Did you know many millionaires drive used vehicles? And even most of those who buy new hold on to them for quite a while. I bought my van used and had it fitted for my chair. New cars depreciate drastically as soon as you drive them off the lot. They continue to lose value each year. I made the financial choice to let others eat that initial depreciation instead of me."

"What do you think about zero-interest car loans?" asked Eddie. "Aren't they okay?"

"You make a good point, Eddie. The responsible use of credit can be part of a healthy financial plan. But everyone's situation is unique, so, I'd recommend discussing that with your advisor. See what they recommend."

Eddie smiled and said, "That's what I'm doing."

Alden laughed. "Good point. I often suggest that my clients pick out their next car, and find out what the payment would be . . ."

"I just did that," said Ayisha. "The car I want would have a zero-interest loan, with a $750 payment for 60 months."

"That's a perfect example," said Alden. "I'll assume you can make the payments comfortably, even after paying yourself first."

Ayisha nodded. "Second, in my case, remember? But yes, that's safe to assume."

"Do you have a car payment now?"

"No."

"Perfect," said Alden. "So, you have a couple of ways to go. Option one is to buy the car and make the payments over 60 months."

"Right." Ayisha nodded.

Alden asked, "Option two is a little different. You continue to drive your current vehicle for those 60 months, but still make that $750 per month car payment."

Ayisha crinkled her nose. "Make that payment to who?"

Alden smiled. "To yourself, Ayisha, as an additional deposit into your investment accounts. Then, at 60 months, take money out and pay cash for your car. At a 10 percent rate of return, you'll buy the car and still have 13,000 additional dollars in your investments that you wouldn't have had otherwise."

Ayisha said, "But car prices will go up during that time."

"True. But you'll likely still come out ahead," said Alden.

"My point is to remember that credit card and high-interest debt will hurt you, rather than help you. I recommend avoiding it."

"But sometimes debt isn't such a bad thing, right?" Eddie said.

Dylan snorted. "So sayeth the banker."

Alden laughed. "There are at least two schools of thought on this. One is you should eliminate all debt. You'll never be financially independent with huge amounts of money owed, especially at very high interest rates. That's the school of thought I prefer."

"What's the other way of thinking?" Yen asked.

"Some suggest having debt only on appreciating assets, such as real estate or business ventures, where your return is high. Others recommend balancing the idea of incurring debt at a low interest rate, so you can keep money in your investment accounts, earning a higher rate of return."

"So how do we know which is the best choice for us?" asked Yen.

Dylan held up his hand. "I got this one, Alden." Deepening his voice, trying to sound older and more refined, he said, "Yen, my dear, you ask your financial advisor."

Alden laughed. "There may be hope for you yet, son."

Ayisha shook her head. "Maybe . . . just maybe." Looking at Dylan, she added, "Not ready to bet on him yet."

Everyone laughed.

Alden said, "That actually brings us to law number six."

6. Invest—save for your future.

"You work hard for your money. Make sure at least some of that money works hard for you, too. Invest each month. Take advantage of any employer-sponsored retirement plans—especially if they match funds. Their contribution is free money to you—an immediate return on your investment. Often, there are helpful tax savings as well. Your financial advisor can guide you on how much to put in, plus additional investment possibilities."

Dylan said, "But what if you don't have any money left over to save or invest?"

Alden laughed. "Go have another beer with Warren Buffett. Remember, invest first, then spend what's left. When you do, you get to take advantage of the wonders of compound interest."

Dylan turned his head slightly and lifted his hands. "Huh? The wonders of what?"

"Compound interest," said Alden.

"When you consistently invest money each month and follow sound advice along the way, you'll usually earn a decent rate of return. When that happens, your investment account is worth more at the end of the year. You'll have what you put in, plus the dollars the account earned. That extra money is your yield."

Dylan said, "Like a farmer getting more corn than they planted . . . their yield, right?"

"Right," said Alden. "Now, imagine the following year, that farmer plants the same amount of seed as the first year, *plus* all of the seed he earned from his yield."

Dylan raised his brow. "He'd start getting a heck of a lot more corn."

Alden smiled. "That's right. That's how compound interest works. You're earning return upon return. It stacks up. The sooner you invest, the more powerful the impact is over the long term."

Ayisha said, "I read an article about that recently, and it shocked me!"

"What'd it say?" asked Cordelia.

"I can't remember the specifics," said Ayisha. "But the point was the earlier you start, the better off you'll be. Drastically better off."

"That's true," Alden said. "I'll give you an example."

He scanned the room. "Let's consider two scenarios."

Alden pointed to Dylan. "First, let's say Dylan invests $5,500 per year, in mutual funds or the stock market, from age 25 to 35. That's 10 years. Then he never invests another dime but allows the account to grow—untouched."

He turned to Eddie. "And second, Eddie invests $5,500 per year but starting at age 35 and continuing to age 65. That's 10 years later and investing for 30 years."

Alden asked the group, "If both men get the exact same 10 percent return on their investments each year, who would have the most money at age 65?"

"Eddie," was the reply from the group.

Cordelia said, "Dylan invests $55,000 over 10 years, and Eddie invests $165,000 over 30 years . . ."

"Wow," Jamie said. "You 'mathed' that in your head? I'm impressed."

Cordelia blushed. "Yes. And I think it would be Eddie who wins."

Alden smiled. "You'd think so, wouldn't you? At age 65, Eddie would have accumulated over $900,000."

Dylan put his hand in the air for a fist bump. "Good job, Eddie!"

Alden said, "But at age 65, Dylan would have over $1.5 million."

Eddie tapped Dylan's fist. "Better job, Dylan!"

"That's incredible," said Ayisha.

"Yes," said Alden. "That's the power of compound interest. Dylan's money was working for 40 years, and Eddie's only 30. That brought Dylan significantly more growth on his investments."

Alden chuckled. "I've seen a quote floating around online—often (probably wrongly) attributed to Albert Einstein—that calls compound interest the eighth wonder of the world. It says, 'He who understands it, earns it. He who doesn't, pays it.' Whether Einstein actually said it or not, the principle is definitely correct."

"What do you mean, pays it?" asked Dylan.

"When you make payments on high-interest debts," said Alden, "someone else is earning compound interest—and *you're* the one paying it. But once you really understand how compound interest works—you start making different choices. You invest, and now *you're* the one earning the return."

"Seriously?" Jamie said, "But can't you lose it all?"

"No investment's without risk. A little uncertainty is inevitable. But if you look at the average rate of return over the last 50 years, the stock market has returned double-digit growth back to investors."

"Get in early. Stay late," Dylan said.

Alden nodded. "Get in now. Then hang in there for the long haul."

"But I don't know how to do any of that," said Cordelia.

ALDEN'S LAWS FOR FINANCIAL INDEPENDENCE

1. Pick a financial pro to mentor you.
2. Pay yourself first.
3. Establish an emergency fund.
4. Budget your spending.
5. Get rid of credit card and high-interest debt.
6. Invest – save for your future.

Abbondanza Pizza

"I'm not so great at it either, Cordelia," Eddie said. "Especially in picking individual stocks. I once bought stock in a donut company. Two months later, the low-carb diet craze hit. The company didn't go out of business, but I lost a lot of money."

Alden said, "That's another reason you should develop a good relationship with a financial professional of your own. They'll spread your money out across multiple sectors, mitigating your risk. They'll tailor a plan to your personal situation."

Eddie wrote on the pizza box.

The lobby phone rang.

Carl answered, tapping his fingers rapidly on the desk.

Gabrielle said, "Hey, Carl. How's it going?"

Carl snarled.

"Oh, it's going well," he growled. "We're just about to turn on the game and break out the beer. Maybe order some wings."

Gabrielle laughed. "Carl, you're cracking me up."

"I'm not seeing anything funny about this, Gabi. What about the plane?"

"We're not going to be able to get a plane here before 4:00. We'll need a bit more time."

He paused for a moment. "Gabi, you need to understand something."

"What, Carl?"

"Make no mistake, I'm losing what little patience I had."

He threw the handset into the cradle.

CHAPTER 14

Multiple Streams, Greater Dreams

3:30 p.m.

Alden heard Carl slam the phone down. He rolled his chair next to Bobby and Jamie and looked into the lobby.

"So, guys, how would you like to see this end? You seem to want to resolve this peacefully. Think you can get Carl to go along?"

"Maybe," said Jamie. "But I know we're going to prison for this. I ain't got *no* interest in doing that!"

Alden looked at Bobby. "You?"

Bobby said nothing at first. Finally, he nodded for Alden and Jamie to move outside the vault. Once they were out of hearing range, Bobby whispered.

"Look. Yes. I want out of this with nobody getting hurt. But I don't know how. You're the expert here. What do you think?"

"Exactly what I said earlier. We let Gabi know what's happening. Everyone else goes out first. Then you guys follow me."

Looking up front, Alden said, "You two need to keep Carl calm, and go convince him to go with this option. If you do, we all finish the day still breathing."

Jamie joined Carl up front while Alden headed toward the vault.

Bobby followed Alden for a couple of steps, then tugged his arm. "For what it's worth, I really wish I'd met you and learned the things you've been talking about years ago. Things might've been different."

Alden said, "Bobby, it's not too late."

Yeah, right.

The afternoon sun shone through the lobby doors, creating a glare that reached all the way into the vault. Fatigue was setting in for those inside and outside the bank.

Gabrielle's job was to keep everyone calm. The SWAT team members were professionals, and not much of a concern. Her efforts focused on those inside the bank. Tired people make mistakes as their stress level rises.

The live video feed showed Carl getting more anxious and erratic. One minute, he was calm. The next, he'd kick a trash can. He paced back and forth.

Bobby and Jamie walked into the vault.

Jamie whispered, "He's losing it."

Bobby said nothing. He positioned himself at the entrance. He leaned back against the opening, his eyes fixed on those inside the vault and out.

Alden kept the group engaged in conversation. The distraction seemed to work.

Cacey waved to get Alden's attention. "Alden, do you believe anyone can do the things you're talking about? Really? Even when they've already messed up in so many ways?"

"I do. Every human has tremendous potential. They just need to be exposed to the possibilities."

"My husband and I don't have anything extra. We've both been out of work for a while. That's why I was in here this morning—applying for a job."

"That does make it tougher, Cacey. Getting a job, or starting a business, has to come first. When I first started working on my relationship with money, I had a job but had no extra funds. I knew I needed to bring in at least a little more if I was going to save and invest."

"So, what'd you do?" Dylan asked.

"I found additional ways to get into the flow of money," said Alden. "I asked for extra shifts. I even started a small business on the side. But here's the key: I didn't spend that surplus. Instead, I saved and invested every single dime."

"That doesn't sound like much fun," said Jamie. "I'd at least want to spend a little extra. Beer money, ya know?"

Alden smiled. "You don't have to cut out everything you find enjoyable. But make room for the idea that better choices will bring you a brighter future. Since I'd started that process decades before I got shot, when that day came, I knew I'd be financially okay."

"Didn't you get a pension?" asked Cordelia.

"I did," said Alden. "But for most people, getting a pension means earning about 60 to 70 percent of what they couldn't live off of already. I'd made the right choices early on, which gave me better options at this stage in my life."

Eddie said, "You know, my father used to say, 'Only a poor mouse has just one hole.'"

"Uh . . . what?" Dylan said.

Eddie laughed. "Mice gather food and bring it back to their various holes for storage. At least that's the way it looks in cartoons. So, they eat out of multiple places. My dad's point was, if you only have one source of income, it's hard to get ahead. So, getting multiple streams of income—more than one hole—is highly desirable."

"How'd you suggest we do that?" asked Dylan.

Alden said, "That often involves a side hustle. If that's in sales, or owning your own business, the best way to earn money is to serve others. Provide value—some tangible benefit. The more people you serve, the more money you make."

"I have a sister who's in direct sales," Cordelia said. "She doesn't make a big profit on each individual item. But over the years, she's developed thousands of regular customers. And even if you only make one dollar per sale, if thousands are buying from you each month . . ."

"Wait!" said Jamie. "I can math on this one for ya." He grinned from ear to ear. "That's thousands of dollars each month!"

Alden laughed. "That's right, Jamie."

Jamie elbowed Bobby. "And my teachers said I was terrible at math!"

"But Alden," said Dylan, "what if you work for somebody else? I can provide tons of value to a boatload of people, but my income in my job is limited by what my boss is willing to pay me."

Alden paused. "I understand what you're saying. I faced a similar limitation during my years in law enforcement. Teachers and government workers do as well."

Ayisha said, "When you think about how much we need police officers and teachers, that doesn't seem quite fair, does it?"

"The fairness," said Alden, "comes with our freedoms. We each have the freedom to change jobs, start and build businesses, and live our lives the way we want. Though those choices may not always be easy or convenient."

"The reality is that different jobs come with different salaries," Eddie said.

Ayisha lifted her hands. "My question is why?"

Alden said, "We all have great intrinsic value—our worth as individuals who live, breathe, love . . . and no one is more valuable than anyone else. But there's a different type of value that comes into play, especially in our career choices. That's market value, and it determines our income."

"Who decides your market value?" Dylan asked.

"Basically," Alden said, "in a free enterprise system such as ours, society and the marketplace does."

"How?" said Dylan.

"It's primarily based on how our work affects the flow of money," said Alden, "and our role in the equation. If we own a business, our product or service brings the money in the door. The more customers we attract, the more money flows in. Then we pay expenses. The rest is our profit . . . our income."

Dylan raised an eyebrow. "And when you're an employee?"

"Paying employees is an expense to the owner," said Alden. "The greater the impact that employee has on increasing revenue, the more they're paid—usually."

Alden turned to Ayisha. "I chose a career in law enforcement. My income wasn't based on my intrinsic value to myself or the community. I loved the job, and it held tremendous meaning for me personally—but since the market value of the job didn't bring in the income I wanted, I decided to do things on the side."

Ayisha said, "Dylan, maybe you could start doing car maintenance for people as a side hustle."

Alden agreed. "That's right. And with many side hustles, you're self-employed. If that's you—find ways to provide value to your customer that's greater than what you take in payment. Your customers become very loyal to you when you do."

"What do you mean? How can I provide more in value than I take in payment and stay in business?" asked Ayisha.

Alden said, "Get creative. It doesn't always have to add to your expenses. Make the patient experience something that is so impressive that it separates you and your team from other doctors in the area. Maybe have a unique waiting room experience that's more enjoyable for patients. Possibly make sure you never have them waiting past their appointment time. Call them after a treatment to check on them, and thank them for choosing you."

"Serve margaritas," said Dylan. "I'd come by once a week!"

"That value doesn't have to be financial." Looking at Dylan, Alden said, "Or booze."

Dylan laughed, "But it don't hurt!"

"In my case," Alden said, "I provide value, making sure my clients enjoy a secure financial future by following my advice. They have a plan in place that creates clarity and confidence. It gives them peace of mind. I collect a small but fair fee for the guidance."

"And your fee is very reasonable," said Eddie.

"Thanks," said Alden. "And since I do that for many clients, it adds up. Their return on investment, plus the peace of mind they receive from the guidance I give, is much greater in value to them than the money they pay me."

Ayisha nodded. "I see now."

Before Alden could say more, a loud crash came from the lobby. Carl had just thrown a chair into the lobby's front window.

Unlock THE VAULT
Secure the combination to access your FREE Resources

Visit **www.HiddenHeistVault.com** to claim your exclusive access to The Vault - a treasure trove of complimentary guides and insights.

*If you experience any difficulty registering for
The Vault, please email* **support@referralcoach.com**

"Financial wealth builds with time. Stay patient, stay the course, and let compounding do its work. Long-term planning turns small steps into big gains."

—Alden Beckett

CHAPTER 15

All Good Things . . .

4:00 p.m.

Although the glass didn't break, the sound got the attention of everyone inside the bank, as well as out front.

Jamie whispered to Bobby. "We've gotta get out of here. I'm gettin' scared."

Bobby said nothing. He just took a quick glance at Cacey.

Carl marched into the vault, his anger the same as when the robbery first began.

"Alright, everybody. Get ready," said Carl. "We're letting all of you go, except one."

Alden looked around the room and said, "It's okay. I'll stay behind . . ."

"Not you!" Pointing to Cacey, Carl said, "Her!"

Carl took steps toward Cacey.

Bobby intercepted him beside Alden's chair, grabbing him by the shirt and pushing him against the wall. He seized the gun from Carl's waist and tucked it into his own belt, behind him, at the small of his back.

Bobby shouted, "I told you, that's not going to happen." Growling at Carl, he said, "The three of us can go on out in a blaze of glory, but you aren't taking . . ." he looked back at his wife, "anybody!"

Carl reached for the gun in his belt, finding nothing.

Bobby tripped Carl, putting him on the floor. He pointed. "Stay down!"

Carl stayed down.

"That's enough," yelled Cacey, in a voice much larger than anyone expected from such a demure young woman.

She walked over to Bobby, and quietly said, "Baby, it's time to stop this."

She reached up to her husband and removed the scarf and glasses from his face. He stood there in disbelief.

"How long have you known?"

"From the beginning, silly. Did you really think I wouldn't recognize my own husband's shoes? How he walks? Heck, half the questions I asked were just so you'd hear the answers."

Hearing the surprise of the others, she turned and said, "Bobby's my husband."

Ayisha scowled. "Were you in on this?"

Before Cacey could answer, Bobby held up his hand. "No. She had no clue."

He looked at his wife. "Were you in here applying for a job?"

Cacey nodded.

Bobby touched her shoulders and brushed the hair from her face. "I can't go to prison. I won't leave you behind to fend for yourself. We have to escape."

Alden said, "Bobby, you're forgetting something."

"What?"

"When you give yourself up, you'll go to prison—for a time. But then you'll get out. You'll be able to come back to Cacey. You'll resume a life with your family."

"I'm *not* going to prison."

"I get that," said Alden. "I don't blame you. But if you go out there and confront the SWAT team, it's gonna go badly."

Alden moved a little closer. "Don't make this choice based on what you want. Make it for Cacey. One way, she may lose you for a few years. The other way . . . she loses you forever."

"Please, Bobby. Don't make me go through that."

Bobby looked at his wife, sighed, and said, "Okay."

He reached behind his waist, retrieved Yen's gun, and handed it to Alden. He then reached into Carl's jacket pocket, pulled out the cell phone, and tossed it over as well.

Alden dialed the phone. Gabrielle answered. "Carl?"

Alden said, "Who, me? Do I look like Carl to you?"

Gabrielle sighed. "I don't know. Have him sit in your lap and text me a picture."

Alden laughed.

"Bobby gave me the gun, after pinning Carl to the wall, then taking him down. You should've seen it. It was impressive."

After a moment, Alden said, "Hey, Gabi?"

"Yep."

"Can you make sure the DA knows . . . without Bobby, this would've been a lot worse."

"Will do."

"Great," said Alden. "We'll head on out now."

"Where are our phones?" said Ayisha. "I need to take pictures of those pizza boxes."

Eddie laughed. "I'll get them."

ALDEN'S SEVEN MONEY TRUTHS

1. We are responsible for our money beliefs and actions — choose wisely.

2. Money isn't scarce, even when it feels like it.

3. Money flows like a river – jump in.

4. Childhood and cultural money messages mislead us — challenge them.

5. Money favors the prepared — get in position to win.

6. Money doesn't grow by accident — learn how it works.

7. Money stereotypes are often wrong – don't blindly believe them.

Abbondanza Pizza

ALDEN'S LAWS FOR FINANCIAL INDEPENDENCE

1. Pick a financial pro to mentor you.
2. Pay yourself first.
3. Establish an emergency fund.
4. Budget your spending.
5. Get rid of credit card and high-interest debt.
6. Invest – save for your future.

Abbondanza Pizza

"Your beliefs about money will either hold you hostage or set you free. The choice is yours."

—Alden Beckett

EPILOGUE

The Best Gift I've Ever Received

Two Years Later

Alden Beckett's office was tastefully decorated with old wooden tables, a leather sofa, and a love seat. In the corners were various decorations and memorabilia of cowboys, Western movies, and two paintings of the Texas Big Bend area.

Hung prominently over the sofa directly opposite the front door: an autographed head shot of John Wayne. Alden had never met The Duke. He bought the framed signed print at a charity auction that raised money for a children's cancer center in Houston.

His clients walked through the front door promptly for their eleven o'clock appointment.

"Hi Alden," said the young woman.

"Hi Cacey," replied Alden. "Hi Bobby! It's good to see you out!"

Bobby said, "It's good to be seen!"

The couple took a seat on the sofa as Alden rolled his chair up beside the coffee table.

Bobby said, "Alden, the first thing I want to say is thank you. Not just for putting a good word in for me at my trial and parole hearing, helping me reduce the sentence. But also for looking in on Cacey while I did my time. I know, thank you isn't really enough. But it's from my heart. I appreciate it."

Alden nodded. "It was my pleasure, Bobby. If you hadn't kept your head on straight during that robbery, it could have ended poorly for all of us. So, thank you too."

Bobby pulled out a leather-bound notebook and handed it to Alden. "I made something to show you."

The book was filled with things Bobby and Cacey had written during his two years in prison. The book's pages were tattered, and its leather worn.

But the notebook was pure gold to Alden.

As he opened the book, the first things he saw, in a plastic pouch, were the stained, torn-out pieces from the two pizza boxes that day. On them were the notes that Eddie had taken.

Alden's Seven Money Truths

1. We are responsible for our money beliefs and actions—choose wisely.
2. Money isn't scarce, even when it feels like it.
3. Money flows like a river—jump in.
4. Childhood and cultural money messages mislead us—challenge them.
5. Money favors the prepared—get in position to win.
6. Money doesn't grow by accident—learn how it works.

7. Money stereotypes are often wrong—don't blindly believe them.

Alden's Laws for Financial Independence

1. Pick a financial pro to mentor you.
2. Pay yourself first.
3. Establish an emergency fund.
4. Budget your spending.
5. Get rid of credit card and high-interest debt.
6. Invest—save for your future.

Alden thumbed through the pages. "This is great, Bobby. But instead of giving it to me, you and Cacey should keep this. Take notes in it as we go through the next years together. I'd rather you have it."

Bobby laughed. "I didn't mean I was giving it to you to keep. I mean, we love you and all, but no . . . we're hanging onto that."

Cacey said, "It's our way of letting you know we hear you. We appreciate you choosing to work with us. And we're going to get this right, with your help."

"That . . ." Alden's voice choked. He took a breath, cleared his throat, and said, "That may be the best gift I've ever received."

Alden finished scanning the notebook and regained his composure. "I'm a little hungry. Would you two like to have lunch? My treat."

"That sounds good," said Bobby. "I was hungry and wanted to grab something on the way over, but Cacey said there wasn't time."

"And we're on a budget," she said.

Alden smiled. "I'm glad she did that. Now we can go together."

Alden locked the doors to his office building, as the three moved outside.

Bobby said, "Do you want us to ride with you in your van, or follow in our car?"

"Neither," said Alden. "We're just going next door."

Alden led the way, taking his chair down the ramp as Bobby and Cacey followed, hand in hand.

In front of the restaurant, Bobby said, "I've never seen this place before."

"It actually opens tomorrow," said Alden. "It's new, but I think I'm going to like it."

Cacey said, "Well you'd better like it, since you own it."

Alden laughed, "So should you, since you manage it."

Bobby leaned back slightly. "What's going on here?"

Cacey said, "Well, you knew I'd been working at a restaurant for the last year. Turns out, I'm pretty good at it . . ."

"Turns out she's actually great at it," Alden interrupted.

Cacey smiled at Alden, then turned back to Bobby.

"So when Alden decided to open up a restaurant as an investment, we talked, and he made me the manager."

"That's great, baby," said Bobby.

He looked up at the sign for the first time.

In bold letters, the sign said, The Vault. The logo was that of an open bank vault, and the neon lights below flashed, Unlock the Secrets of Great Food.

Bobby laughed. "Gee, Alden. I wonder where you came up with that catchy name?"

Alden said, "You haven't seen the half of it. All the booths and tables are themed—some as vaults, and others as jail cells. And the waitstaff can dress in any character that fits with the central idea."

Bobby pulled on the front door. "I can't wait to see inside."

It took a few seconds for his eyes to adjust to the change in light from the sunny parking lot to the darker shade of the lobby.

As the three moved into the main dining area, Bobby saw a banner hanging on the wall; it said, Welcome Home Bobby.

Ayisha, Dylan, Cordelia, Yen, and Eddie shouted, "Surprise!"

Startled, Bobby said, "Wow. Thanks everybody." He let out a slow sigh and lowered his head. "But after what happened, I can't believe this."

Alden said, "Like I said, Bobby, this could have ended very badly if it weren't for you. We all know that. Yes, you made a big mistake. But you've paid your price and now have a supportive group of friends to help you move forward."

Dylan said, "Yeah, and besides, if you hadn't done that, I would've never met Alden. He's helping me now, too."

Alden smirked. "You're still a work in progress, son."

Everyone laughed.

Eddie lifted his glass. "He's helping all of us now."

The others raised their glasses as well.

Bobby looked around the room, his eyes dampening and voice cracking. He squeezed Cacey's hand and said, "Thank you. Thank you everyone."

THE END

Unlock THE VAULT
And Your Financial Independence

Secure the **combination** to access your FREE Resources

Visit **HiddenHeistVault.com**
to claim your exclusive access to
The Vault - a treasure trove of guides
and insights designed to help you:

- Enrich your money mindset
- Grow lasting personal wealth
- Avoid financial regrets
- Move toward financial freedom

Inside The Vault, you will discover powerful resources like:

- 9 Strategies to Grow and Protect Your Financial Future
- How Ordinary People Become Millionaires
- 13 Important Things You Can Do With Money
- Can Money Buy Happiness? Think Twice
- The Ever-Flowing River of Money
- Creating Generational Wealth
- **Behind the Scenes: Interviews with Bill, Jeff, and some special guests who... well...let's just say have first-hand experience in the world of hostage negotiations.**

Your journey to a wiser, wealthier life starts here.

 Go to **www.HiddenHeistVault.com** to unlock the combination today!

APPENDIX I

Limiting Beliefs, Mistaken Assumptions, and Unhelpful Emotions

Unhelpful beliefs, assumptions, and attitudes toward money may keep you from establishing financial wellness, building wealth, and achieving financial freedom. Remember, not everything you think—or everything you believe—is true. Be willing to question the stories you tell yourself.

Common Examples:
1. **Money is a scarce resource.**
Money is abundant and dynamic, constantly flowing through the economy. While your access may be limited, banks lend deposits to businesses, fueling jobs and innovation globally. Understanding this flow helps you position yourself to benefit from its abundance.

2. **Making money is a zero-sum game (if I make more, someone else makes less).**

Related to the above belief, the idea that making money is a zero-sum game is limiting. A scarcity mindset fuels competition, while an abundance mindset fosters collaboration and growth. Expanding wealth creates opportunities, benefiting everyone.

See The Vault for more information on how money flows: www.HiddenHeistVault.com

3. **Money is the root of all evil.**

This verse is often misquoted. The Bible says, "The love of money is the root of all evil" (1 Timothy 6:10, KJV), warning against an unhealthy attachment that leads to moral compromise. Misinterpreting this verse may create guilt around wealth, but when money is used to help others, enrich life, and provide independence, it aligns with a clear conscience.

As Eddie said in Chapter 9, "We should *use* money—and *love* people. Greed and crime occur when we do the opposite."

4. **I'm not good with money.**

This mindset can become a self-fulfilling prophecy, leading to poor financial habits. Instead, seek financial education—learn the basics of saving, investing, budgeting, and debt. Knowledge boosts confidence and transforms how you manage money.

5. **I feel shame about money.**

Money shame is a common, painful emotion linking self-worth to finances, fueled by cultural norms, social comparisons, and past struggles. It can cause embarrassment, avoidance, or harmful spending habits. With the right support (counseling or coaching) it can be reduced or overcome.

See "The Vault" for more on this important topic.

6. **You have to have money to make money.**

This statement isn't totally false. Starting a business requires capital. Taking advantage of the dynamic of compounding requires at least an initial amount invested. However, this belief becomes a problem when it's used as an excuse to avoid pursuing options like saving, investing, and exploring strategic partnerships.

7. **Rich people are entitled, greedy, dishonest, lucky, or corrupt. (Name your negative adjective.)**

As is the problem with any stereotype, Alden expresses the reality in Chapter 9: "Some are. Most aren't."

If we believe this, building wealth becomes difficult as our actions conflict with our subconscious beliefs. Cognitive dissonance makes it nearly impossible to become what we despise, leading to fear of wealth or resentment toward the wealthy. It's hard to become what you resent.

8. **Poor people are lazy.**

Like the point above, some are, but most aren't. Many hardworking people struggle due to limited skills or lack of role models. Financial education and a vision for success, often through mentorship and role models, can help break these barriers.

9. **I don't really care about money. Money is not important to me.**
Sometimes, this reflects true values, but it can also be an excuse to avoid financial challenges. While it may ease stress, it can also limit opportunities for growth and wealth.

10. **I don't deserve to be wealthy.**
Some people feel undeserving due to past mistakes with money or because of messages they received while growing up. Clearly, this will hinder one's ability to take any action that may bring more money into their life.

11. **Money can't buy happiness.**
Money doesn't guarantee lasting happiness but improves quality of life by reducing stress and providing opportunities for experiences. True happiness, however, comes from relationships, growth, and feelings of purpose and acceptance.

12. **You can't be rich and have a good work-life balance.**
Wealth and work-life balance aren't mutually exclusive. Some sacrifice time for wealth, while others succeed through smart management and investments. Financial resources can provide flexibility for hobbies, family, and well-being—balance depends on personal choices.

13. **Earning money should be hard—is a struggle.**
This belief can cause people to dismiss easy opportunities, feel guilty about high earnings, or self-sabotage. Accepting that wealth can come in various ways expands opportunities and accelerates financial independence.

14. I missed the boat or I'm too old to start.

Time matters in building wealth, but it's never too late to start. Investing, entrepreneurship, and better financial habits can create success at any age.

Arianna Huffington: Launched *The Huffington Post* at age 55.

Momofuku Ando: invented instant ramen noodles at age 57 (Nisson Foods).

Jody Boyman: Co-founded Hungry Planet, a plant-based meat company, at age 60.

Lisa Skeete Tatum: Founded Landit, a career development platform, at age 47.

Colonel Harland Sanders: Founded Kentucky Fried Chicken (KFC) at age 62.

Ray Kroc: Started franchising McDonald's at age 52.

15. If I earn more money, I'll be in a higher tax bracket and that's bad.

The idea that earning more is bad due to higher taxes is a misconception. In the U.S., only income within a higher bracket is taxed at that rate, so a raise always increases take-home pay. While higher earnings may affect some benefits, the financial gain usually outweighs any drawbacks.

16. All debt is bad.

While carrying a balance on high-interest consumer and credit card debt definitely hurts your financial future, the notion that all debt is bad is an oversimplification. When strategically used, some debt is worth considering. For instance, a home mortgage can provide a stable place to live while building equity, and a low-interest loan can, in certain situations, allow you to buy a car or invest in a project while keeping most of your money compounding in sound investments.

17. **Money is power. People use money to control others.**
Money holds power, influencing decisions and behaviors. While some may use it to control, others use it to fund meaningful and effective charities. Money itself is neutral—its impact (good or bad) depends on how it's used.

Unlock THE VAULT
Secure the combination to access your FREE Resources

Visit **www.HiddenHeistVault.com** to claim your exclusive access to The Vault - a treasure trove of complimentary guides and insights.

If you experience any difficulty registering for The Vault, please email **support@referralcoach.com**

APPENDIX II

Wealthy Mindset and Action Steps for Financial Independence

Our story focused on limiting money beliefs, but wealth-building also requires an expansive, abundant mindset.

1. **Money as a Force for Good**
Money itself is neutral—it amplifies intentions. Used wisely, it can support loved ones, fund charities, and create opportunities.
   Action Step: Use your money this month to make a positive impact.

2. **Define Your Financial Freedom**
Freedom means having enough resources to live on your terms—not necessarily luxury, but control and choice.
   Action Step: Define your financial freedom in detail. What does it look, feel, and even smell like?

3. Protect Your Wealth

Accumulating wealth is only part of the equation; protecting it matters too.

Action Step: Consult a financial advisor on insurance and risk protection.

4. Pay Yourself First

Save before you spend. Automating savings makes it effortless.

Action Step: Set up automatic transfers to a high-yield savings or retirement account.

5. Fund Your Dreams

Unfunded dreams stay dreams. To make them reality, prioritize them financially.

Action Step: Start a dedicated savings or investment account for personal or family goals.

6. Money as a Magnifier

Money doesn't change you—it reveals you.

Action Step: Reflect on how your spending aligns with your values. Adjust as needed.

7. Follow the Money

Your financial habits reveal your true priorities.

Action Step: Audit your spending. Does it reflect what matters most to you?

8. The Power of Compounding

Small, consistent investments grow exponentially. (At a 5 percent annual interest rate, compounded monthly, investing $500/month from age 30 to 65 grows to about $570,000. With professional guidance, returns could be even higher.)

Action Step: Start investing in an account with compound interest—now.

9. Diversify for Security

Putting all your resources in one area increases risk. Spreading your investments over different products and platforms reduces risk.

Action Step: Review your portfolio for diversification. Seek expert advice if needed.

10. Purposeful Spending

Research has revealed that experiences contribute more significantly to happiness and well-being than material goods.

Action Step: For the next gift you give to yourself or someone else, consider an experience over an object.

11. The Power of Spending Habits

Building wealth isn't just about income, it's also about outflow; about how well you manage money.

Action Step: Track your spending for 30 days to find saving opportunities.

12. Break Free from Expensive Debt

Debt should be strategic, not limiting.

Action Step: Seek financial guidance about what type of debit might help you further your goals without limiting your wealth-building.

13. Generational Wealth Thinking

Leaving money to future generations creates financial dignity and even financial security.

Action Step: Work with an advisor on estate planning, trusts, and educational funds.

14. Financial Education Matters

Knowledge is the foundation of smart decisions and long-term wealth. Understanding money leads to better decisions.

Action Step: Learn one new financial concept weekly.

15. Time Beats Timing

Long-term investments in the stock market and other investments typically outperform attempts to predict short-term fluctuations. For most people, trying to "time the market" is a fool's errand that will lose money over the long run.

Action Step: Commit to consistent saving and investing. Employ dollar-cost averaging.

16. The Buck Stops with You

Financial success requires active involvement, not blind delegation.

Action Step: If you suspect your advisor isn't truly acting in your best interest, reassess the relationship. Get a second opinion.

17. What You Focus on Grows Stronger in Your Life

Direct your attention toward financial opportunities, not just problems.

Action Step: Start each day with a positive money affirmation.

APPENDIX III

Eight Strategies to Grow and Protect Your Financial Future

Building a secure financial future requires saving, investing, managing debt, and planning for the unexpected. Use this guide to navigate conversations with a financial professional to grow, protect, and achieve financial independence.

1. **Establish an Emergency Fund**
What to Do: Save three to six months' worth of essential living expenses in a high-yield savings account.
Why It Matters: Life happens—unexpected bills or job loss. An emergency fund is your safety net, allowing you to avoid debt.
Action Tip: Automate your savings by setting up recurring transfers to your emergency fund. Out of sight, out of mind (until needed).

2. Pay Off High-Interest Debt First

What to Do: Tackle debts with high interest rates (like credit cards and consumer loans) before those with lower interest rates (such as student loans).

Why It Matters: High-interest debt drains wealth. Paying it off frees money to save and invest.

Action Tip: For high-interest debt, use the snowball (smallest first) or avalanche (highest rate first) method—whichever keeps you motivated.

3. Start Investing Early*

What to Do: Begin as soon as you can, even with small amounts, by contributing to employer-sponsored plans—like a 401(k)—or opening an Individual Retirement Account (IRA). Use a Roth IRA. Consult with a professional.

Why It Matters: Start early—compound interest helps your money grow, like a tree gaining strength over time.

Action Tip: Don't wait until you "have more money." Even $25 a week can grow impressively over time!

4. Obtain Adequate Insurance Coverage

What to Do: Ensure you have health, life, and disability insurance, and long-term care insurance. If you have dependents, life insurance is especially critical.

Why It Matters: Insurance protects you from financial devastation during life's big disruptions. A single hospital visit can cost thousands without coverage.

---

* There is a difference between saving and investing. Generally speaking, saving is for short-term needs in low-risk accounts, while investing aims for long-term growth with higher risk. Consult a financial professional for the right mix.

Action Tip: Review your policies annually to ensure they still meet your needs (things change and you might forget). Insurance costs money; however, consider the cost of doing nothing.

5. **Contribute to Retirement Accounts**

What to Do: Maximize your contributions to accounts like 401(k)s and IRAs. Always take full advantage of employer matching—it's essentially free money.

Why It Matters: These accounts offer tax benefits and compound growth potential, helping you prepare for a comfortable retirement.

Action Tip: Increase your contributions whenever you get a raise—you won't even notice the difference in your paycheck.

6. **Gain Financial Literacy**

What to Do: Read books, take workshops, or follow well-respected and credible financial resources. Be careful not to accept television personalities as the ultimate authority. Their advice is often generic in nature and may or may not apply to you.

Why It Matters: The more you know, the better decisions you will make. Financial literacy puts you in control of your money instead of feeling controlled by it.

Action Tip: Start with books by Ric Edelman such as *The Truth About Money* and *The Truth About Your Future.*

7. **Set Clear Financial Goals**

What to Do: Define specific, measurable goals, like saving $20,000 for a down payment in three years or paying off a $5,000 credit card balance in 12 months.

Why It Matters: Clear goals give you focus and motivation. They also make it easier to track progress and celebrate milestones.

Action Tip: Break big goals into smaller steps to stay motivated—progress adds up! Start funding those goals now. Without financing, they are merely dreams.

8. **Review Regularly and Adjust Accordingly**
What to Do: Revisit your financial goals and strategies annually—or after major life events (like getting married or starting a new job).
Why It Matters: Life evolves, and your financial plan should too. Adjusting ensures you stay on track despite changes in your income, expenses, or priorities.
Action Tip: Schedule a "money date" to review finances yearly or more. Even if you plan to do your financial planning mostly without help, get an advisor's second opinion.

Final Thoughts
By embracing these strategies, you're taking control of your financial life—step by step. It's not about being perfect; it's about being consistent. Celebrate small wins, stay curious, and keep moving forward. Your future self (and future generations) will thank you!

Unlock THE VAULT

And Your Financial Independence

Secure the **combination** to access your **FREE Resources**

Visit **HiddenHeistVault.com**
to claim your exclusive access to
The Vault - a treasure trove of guides
and insights designed to help you:

- Enrich your money mindset
- Grow lasting personal wealth
- Avoid financial regrets
- Move toward financial freedom

Inside The Vault, you will discover powerful resources like:

- 9 Strategies to Grow and Protect Your Financial Future
- How Ordinary People Become Millionaires
- 13 Important Things You Can Do With Money
- Can Money Buy Happiness? Think Twice
- The Ever-Flowing River of Money
- Creating Generational Wealth
- **Behind the Scenes: Interviews with Bill, Jeff, and some special guests who... well...let's just say have first-hand experience in the world of hostage negotiations.**

Your journey to a wiser, wealthier life starts here.

 Go to **www.HiddenHeistVault.com**
to unlock the combination today!

ABOUT THE AUTHORS

Bill Cates and Jeff C. West

Bill Cates, CSP, CPAE, believes that everyone deserves to make educated financial decisions that are in their best interest. Bill has turned this belief into his mission—to bring financial education to as many people as he can reach.

For over 30 years, Bill has helped financial professionals and businesses move from incremental growth to exponential growth by communicating more compelling value, balancing digital and human marketing strategies, multiplying their best clients through referrals, and targeting profitable niche markets.

He is the author of seven books, the founder of *The Cates Academy for Relationship Marketing*™, and the host of the acclaimed *Top Advisor Podcast*, ranked in the top 5 percent of podcasts worldwide. Bill was inducted into the Professional Speakers Hall of Fame in 2010.

Bill is also somewhat of an adventurer. He has trekked through the Himalayas of Nepal. He has lived on a houseboat in Kashmir India, reached the summit of Mt. Kilimanjaro, camped in the Arctic

Circle, cycled through Vietnam . . . and has toured the country as the drummer in a rock and roll band.

To tap into Bill's goldmine of free, business-building resources, go to www.ReferralCoach.com/resources.

Jeff C. West is an acclaimed author of business parables, including *The Unexpected Tour Guide, Said the Lady with the Blue Hair* (coauthored with Lisa M. Wilber), and *Streetwise to Saleswise* (coauthored with Bob Burg). His storytelling approach has made complex sales and leadership principles both accessible and impactful, earning his books six distinguished awards—much to his delight and, perhaps, to the surprise of his former college English professors.

Before becoming an author, Jeff spent over 30 years building a successful career in sales and leadership, spanning industries from musical instruments to employee benefit programs. His leadership guided teams to over $150 million in recurring revenue sales.

A native of Georgia, and now a proud Texan, Jeff once played professionally in a Dixieland band—because, as he likes to say, "Everyone loves the tuba player."

If *The Hidden Heist* stole your attention, Jeff C. West's newsletter will keep you hooked—with behind-the-scenes glimpses into his life as an author and practical advice on sales and leadership that you can actually use—all drawn from his decades of real-world experience.

To sign up, go to: www.jeffcwest.com.

www.ingramcontent.com/pod-product-compliance
Lightning Source LLC
Chambersburg PA
CBHW030322080526
44584CB00012B/671